Commodity
Risk Management
and Finance

Commodity Risk Management and Finance

Theophilos Priovolos and Ronald C. Duncan, Editors

Published for the World Bank
Oxford University Press

Oxford University Press

OXFORD NEW YORK TORONTO DELHI
BOMBAY CALCUTTA MADRAS KARACHI
PETALING JAYA SINGAPORE HONG KONG
TOKYO NAIROBI DAR ES SALAAM
CAPE TOWN MELBOURNE AUCKLAND
and associated companies in
BERLIN IBADAN

Manufactured in the United States of America
First printing June 1991

The text of this book is printed on paper containing
50 percent virgin pulp, 45 percent recycled preconsumer waste,
and 5 percent recycled and deinked postconsumer waste.

Library of Congress Cataloging-in-Publication Data

Commodity risk management and finance / edited by Theophilos Priovolos and
Ronald C. Duncan.
    p.   cm.
"Published for the World Bank."
Includes bibliographical references and index.
ISBN 0-19-520867-6
    1. Commodity-backed bonds. 2. Debts. External–Developing
countries. I. Priovolos, Theophilos. II. Duncan, Ronald C.,
1936–. III. International Bank for Reconstruction and Development.
HG4651.C694   1991   90-25115
332.63'23–dc20   CIP

Foreword

As has been made painfully obvious during the 1980s, the developing countries face great difficulties in raising external finance and in servicing their external debts, due in large part to the sharp fluctuations in the prices received for their primary commodity exports. Their terms of trade are also very susceptible to import price shocks, especially from the most important primary commodity import for most of them—petroleum. In turn, the terms-of-trade shocks from primary commodity price fluctuations are a major problem for the management of firms and, probably most important, for the macroeconomic management of the developing countries themselves. It is probably fair to say that the effort that has had to be devoted to macro management of these economies in the wake of such shocks has detracted seriously from the effort that would have otherwise been given to getting on with the process of development.

As the chapters in this volume show, there are now commodity price-related financial instruments that can be used to manage the volatility in export earnings and import payments and to shift the risks from the developing countries to those more capable of bearing them in world markets. As a result, revenue and expenditure streams can be made more stable, debt servicing can be made more reliable, creditworthiness can be improved, and macroeconomic management can be made less onerous.

The use of commodity price-related instruments for hedging commodity price risks and for raising finance has expanded rapidly in recent years in industrial countries. Their use has been minimal in developing countries, however, in part because they are new, but also because of the lack of understanding by the countries of their risk exposure and lack of knowledge about private market-based risk management practices. This lack of knowledge presents an opportunity for the World Bank Group to

v

provide technical assistance to developing countries. A unit has been formed in the International Economics Department to undertake such technical assistance to make developing countries, institutions, and enterprises that face substantial commodity price risk more aware of commodity price-related instruments; to help them obtain training and experience in the use of the various risk management instruments available; and to help them to develop appropriate strategies for commodity risk management. Technical assistance of this nature is presently being undertaken in several countries.

D. C. Rao
Director,
International Economics Department
The World Bank

Contents

Contributors

Ronald Anderson, Department des Sciences Economiques, Universite Catholique de Louvain, Belgium

Richard J. Ball, Department of Agricultural and Research Economics, University of California, Berkeley

Stijn Claessens, Debt and International Finance Division, World Bank

Ronald C. Duncan, International Trade Division, World Bank

Moctar A. Fall, Capital Markets Group, Salomon Brothers Inc., New York

Christopher Gilbert, Department of Economics, Queen Mary and Westfield College, London

Robert J. Myers, Department of Agricultural Economics, Michigan State University, East Lansing

David Newbery, Department of Applied Economics, University of Cambridge

Andrew Powell, Department of Economics, Queen Mary and Westfield College, London

Theophilos Priovolos, Elf Trading S.A., Geneva

Raghuram Rajan, Sloane School of Management, Massachusetts Institute of Technology, Boston

Stanley R. Thompson, Department of Agricultural Economics, Michigan State University, East Lansing

Brian Wright, Department of Agricultural and Research Economics, University of California, Berkeley

Acknowledgments

We owe a substantial debt to the colleagues who have contributed their papers to this volume. Special thanks also go to Don Lessard and Todd Petzel who commented on several of the papers in the book and to the three anonymous reviewers of the Editorial Committee of the World Bank. We also thank the copyright owners of reproduced articles in the book who gave permission to reprint the articles and the American Economic Association and American Agricultural Economics Association for allowing us to present several of these articles at their December 1988 Conference in New York. We are grateful for the financial support of the World Bank and, in particular, of its Research Committee. We acknowledge with many thanks the encouragement and support of Stanley Fischer, chief economist of the World Bank when this volume was written, for the risk management work in the International Commodity Markets Division.

We have also benefited from the comments and suggestions of a number of others in the World Bank Group, including Jean Baneth, David Bock, Kemal Dervis, Ishac Diwan, Enrique Domenge, Robert Graffam, Ishrat Husain, Ronald Johannes, Peter Jones, Ruben Lamdany, Charles Larkum, Johannes Linn, Carl Ludvik, Herbert Morais, Barbara Opper, Sanjivi Rajasingham, Lester Seigel, Andrew Steer, John Taylor, Anthony Toft, John Underwood, Frank Vita, Dimitri Vittas, and all our colleagues in the International Commodity Markets Division. In addition, we would like to thank Gerry Pollio of Chemical Bank; Gaylen Byker and John Grobstein of Paribas; Tony Singleton and Sykes Wilford of Chase Manhattan Bank; Neil Thalheim of Bankers Trust; Srini Vasan of First Boston; Ian Giddy and Frank Ocwieja of Drexel; Viktor Filatov of Morgan Guaranty; Bob Hormatz, John Goldberg, Mike Schwerin, and Tom Demeure of Goldman Sachs and J. Aron; John Rinaldi, Heinz xiiCOMMODITY RISK MANAGEMENT AND FINANCE

Binder, Dietrich Schimelbush, and John Murmann of Metallgesellschaft; Janik Lecamp of Cargill; Mark Adams of McInsey; Eduardo Schwartz of the University of California at Los Angeles; Peter Woodward of Mase-Westpac; Tim Besley of Princeton University; and Cliff Lewis of the U.S. Agency for International Development.

We also acknowledge our appreciation for the superb secretarial assistance of Julie Carroll.

1

Introduction

Theophilos Priovolos and Ronald C. Duncan

Developing countries are exposed to major financial risks and, in particular, to commodity price risks. Their exposure to these risks and their limited ability to deal with the risks effectively was obvious in the 1980s, when sustained declines in commodity prices and sharp increases in interest rates were followed by increases in indebtedness and debt-servicing difficulties.

One form of financing that has expanded greatly in the financial markets of industrial countries in the second half of the 1980s and that appears to offer considerable potential for risk management in developing countries is commodity-linked financing. This book brings together a series of papers that examines the various uses of commodity-linked financing by entities in industrial countries and analyzes the merits of their use in developing countries.

The exposure of developing countries to instability in commodity prices is illustrated in table 1-1 by their dependence on commodity exports. This dependence is the highest in Africa, Oceania, and Latin America, while less so in Asia and southern Europe. The share of commodity exports accounts for 42 percent of developing country exports, but only 25 percent of industrial country exports. The exchange rate and interest rate exposure of developing countries is illustrated in figure 1-1, with information on the debt composition of developing countries. Most public and publicly guaranteed debt is still in U.S. dollars, although increasingly less so since 1982. The shares of U.K. pound, Japanese yen and German deutsche mark (DM) public and publicly guaranteed debt are increasing. These four currencies account for almost all borrowing by developing countries. The noted shift in the past 10 years toward borrowing at variable interest rates underlines the dependence of developing countries on interest rates in the United States,

Table 1-1 *Share of Exports of 33 Primary Commodities from Developing Countries by Region, 1982–84 Average* (number of countries)

Region	Share of exports (percent)				
	0–25	*25–30*	*50–75*	*75–100*	*Total*
Latin America	3	10	11	3	27
Africa	6	13	10	14	43
Asia	8	5	3	3	19
Oceania	0	1	2	1	4
Southern Europe	5	0	0	0	5
Total	22	29	26	21	98

Source: World Bank, 1988a.

United Kingdom, Japan, and Germany. The following two examples illustrate the difficulties that many developing countries faced in the 1980s in managing their commodity exposure.

Coffee, bananas, and beef account for 50 percent of total Costa Rican exports. This country was hit by a series of severe trade shocks from 1978 to 1982. These shocks resulted from falling prices in its major export commodities. The initial response appears to have been to treat the downturn in export earnings as temporary and borrow externally to maintain domestic consumption and investment levels. With the onset of the debt crisis in 1981, however, this strategy was no longer sustainable. The ensuing restrictions on new external borrowing precipitated a disastrous economic slump that began around 1981 and continued to 1983. Costa Rica has become a highly indebted country; at present, its growth potential is handicapped by its debt-servicing requirements. The secondary market for Costa Rican debt, which trades at a large discount, reflects the market's perception of Costa Rica's ability to service its debt. To ensure that the country does not return to a debt-burdened situation will require a debt reduction scheme, such as the Brady Plan, accompanied by good macroeconomic management and the implementation of hedging programs.

In Algeria, there was a substantial trade shock in 1986 with the decline in oil prices. Algeria's hydrocarbon exports account for some 90 percent of total exports. In this case too, the country tried to stabilize its consumption path by borrowing from abroad. In contrast to the Costa Rican situation, the Algerian economy (despite reaching a higher level of indebtedness than in the past) has been able to absorb the impact of the shock to its terms of trade. Nevertheless, the oil shock has alerted the authorities to the vulnerability of the economy to the variability of hydrocarbon prices and to the need to hedge the downside exposure of the economy to reduce the chances of a future deterioration in growth.

Although for some developing countries (in particular, those that are highly indebted) the first priority is to reduce their indebtedness, almost all need to maintain sound macroeconomic policies—including implementation of effective risk management programs. There are, in fact, many commodity risk management instruments available to developing countries. They can be categorized into three groups: self-insurance instruments, third party insurance instruments, and other instruments.

The first group includes instruments such as reserve management schemes, domestic stabilization schemes, macroeconomic policies, and

Figure 1-1 *Currency Composition of Public and Publicly Guaranteed Developing Country Debt*

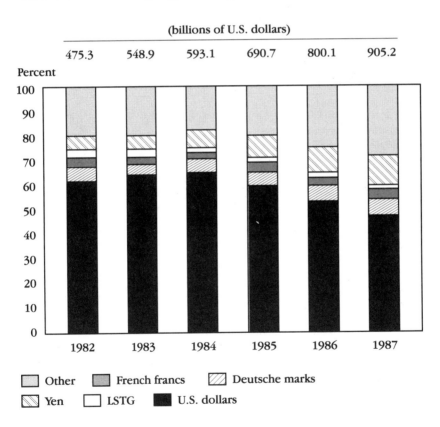

Source: World Bank (1988).

diversification programs. The second group includes financial market instruments such as futures, forwards, options, swaps, and long-term contracts, among others. The third group includes all other schemes such as international commodity agreements and compensatory financing schemes, including the STABEX/SYSMIN schemes of the European Economic Community (EEC), for example.

One instrument that combines risk management with finance, whose use has greatly expanded in the late 1980s, is commodity-linked financing. This financial market instrument (belonging to the second group of risk management instruments) can help industrial and developing countries alike raise funds, while linking revenues with expenses and assets with liabilities. Commodity-linked financing is a hybrid instrument: It is a risk management instrument as well as a financing instrument. As commodity-linked financings extend beyond one year, their risk management properties are of strategic importance to the commodity price exposures of the organizations involved. Commodity-linked financing comes in many forms, such as commodity bonds, commodity loans, and others.

The chapters in Part I cover the issue of the pricing of commodity-linked securities. Chapter 2 reviews the different forms of commodity-linked financing. A conventional bond makes semiannual coupon payments, determined by a coupon rate, and pays out the principal amount at maturity. The nominal return to the investor is known, but, with the uncertainty of the inflation rate over time, the real return is uncertain. With commodity bonds, investors have sought to link their investment to real assets. Commodity bonds exist in two different forms: those of a forward type, often called convertible or indexed bonds, and those of the option or warrant type. In commodity bonds of the forward type, the coupon and/or principal payments are linked to a stated quantity of a commodity. A commodity bond of the option type makes normal coupon payments (just as conventional bonds do), but, upon maturity, the holder of these bonds has, in addition to the principal, the option to buy or sell a predetermined quantity of the commodity at a predetermined price. Because of the inherent value of such an option, the coupon payments of this bond are lower than they would be in a conventional bond.

Use of these instruments goes back at least a century. There has been a recent awakening of interest in commodity-linked bonds, however, building in late 1986 and 1987. Several dozens of commodity bonds (most linked to gold, silver, and oil) have been issued, at an approximate value of US$3 billion–4 billion. Most have been issued in the Euromarkets because of uncertainty about the U.S. regulatory environment. Since the October 1987 stock market crash, however, the retreat of institutional investors from the Euromarkets has led to a reduction in the volume of commodity-linked bonds issued in those markets.

The decline of commodity bond issues has been compensated by a dramatic increase in the number and volume of commodity loans and private commodity bond and note placements. Because commodity loans and private placements are less transparent, the volume of commodity-linked financing is unknown. Commercial banks estimate the volume to be in excess of US$4 billion per annum.

The demand for commodity bonds comes from speculators and hedgers. Chapter 3 discusses a theoretical model of the demand for commodity bonds. This is an extension of the work done by O'Hara (1984). O'Hara showed that if commodity bonds are priced fairly, they will be demanded only if there is a minimum necessary consumption quantity or the bond's payoff negatively correlates with the individual's portfolio return. The bond is valuable because it provides a form of insurance in hedging risks of future consumption. In chapter 3, Fall shows that the demand function for commodity bonds has two components, a speculative component and a hedging component, and that the demand for commodity bonds is positive when the investor has a lower relative modified risk tolerance than the market (i.e., a higher relative modified risk aversion).

In part I, different approaches to pricing commodity bonds are discussed in chapters 4 and 5. A review of the Schwartz (1982) method is presented by Priovolos in chapter 4. The Schwartz model considers the impact on bond pricing of commodity risk, default risk, and interest rate risk. In chapter 5, Rajan bypasses the mathematical complications of the Schwartz model when default risk is introduced by the use of binomial pricing theory. Neither of these chapters considers sovereign risk, however. The introduction of such risk is particularly important for developing countries, and it is discussed in the last chapter of part II.

There are five chapters in part II. The issues addressed in this section provide insights on three levels: those that apply to commodity-linked finance whether or not the borrower is a sovereign with the related limitations of contract enforceability, those that apply to a sovereign with a clean financial slate, and those that apply to sovereign borrowing in the presence of an existing debt overhang. The chapter by Myers and Thompson focuses on the first level, computing commodity hedge ratios for a country facing variance in commodity output, as well as in the price of its commodity exports. They derive the optimal conditions for the use of commodity bonds of the forward type in a hedge of the external debt requirements of a hypothetical commodity-dependent country. In chapter 7, Claessens introduces exchange rate risk, in addition to commodity price risk, in hedging external debt requirements.

The next two chapters by Ball and Myers and Wright and Newbery make important contributions at the first two levels. In chapter 8, Ball and Myers extend the analysis by Thompson and Myers to a sovereign with a clean financial slate. In chapter 9, Wright and Newbery, without reference to the limits of enforceability, quantify the magnitude and welfare costs of export revenue variance for countries characterized by concentrated exports. They also analyze and quantify the relative performance of reserve management versus commodity hedging in reducing fluctuations in the foreign income of such countries. Estimates of the cost of price variability and the potential benefits from risk reduction as a result of employing these two mechanisms clearly demonstrate the importance of risk management. Wright and Newbery also show, within the context of sovereign borrowing, the way in which alternative types of commodity-linked contracts affect the probability of default and, hence, access to external finance in an idealized rational world.

In chapter 10, Anderson, Gilbert, and Powell begin with the problem of sovereign borrowing and the comparative advantage of lenders in bearing particular forms of risk. They find that the required insurance premiums for guaranteeing sovereign risk are minimized when the insuring body has a comparative advantage in bearing sovereign risk and when the contractual terms of any new financing are contingent on factors affecting the borrower's present and future earnings. They show that assets that are contingent on commodity prices may be the most suitable form of obligation for many developing countries. Commodity bonds and loans, long-term commodity options, forwards, and swaps have proliferated in the developed countries in the past few years. The liquidity of these commodity-risk management instruments, although still not comparable to that of similar foreign exchange or interest rate instruments, is growing at a very fast pace. Why is it then that developing countries do not hedge their commodity exposure with these financial instruments? In part, it is because developing country organizations (with the exception of some multinational organizations) do not have the knowledge or the institutional basis to hedge their short-term operational and long-term strategic commodity exposure. Moreover, the hedging cost for developing countries is substantially higher than that of industrial countries. This is due to the perceived sovereign risk of developing countries.

While chapters 6 and 7 address the issue of how much of one's exposure to hedge, chapters 8–10 explore the reasons commodity-linked finance is important for program and project finance in developing countries. Here it is shown that the two parts of commodity finance—risk management and finance—can be structured in such a way that they maximize the welfare (however defined) of an organization. Furthermore, in chapter 10, it is shown that within a debt restructuring framework, where negative pledge clauses could be waived, the sovereign risk assumed by a commercial bank with a properly structured commodity-linked bond or loan is much less than with a conventional bond or loan. In other words, the capital of a bank can be better used when its clients commit to hedge their commodity exposure with properly structured commodity loans. In turn, the bank would have to hedge its commodity price exposure in the financial markets, where it is presumed to do so at a lesser cost than its clients.

The final chapter summarizes the findings in this volume and addresses the costs and benefits of commodity-contingent financing instruments, from the viewpoint of both the issuer and the investor. Finally, the possible role of international development agencies in this area of development finance is discussed.

PART I

The Pricing of Commodity-Linked Securities

2

Experience with Commodity-Linked Issues

Theophilos Priovolos

In response to the appetite of investors eager to participate in the possible upswing of long-underperforming commodities and in response to the risk management needs of primary commodity producers—in particular, precious metal producers—commodity-linked securities proliferated in the late 1980s. Securities linked to the prices of silver, gold, and oil were particularly popular with investors. Almost all commodity-linked financings were issued by corporations and governments in the developed world. In developing countries, however, very few offerings occurred. This chapter reviews recent experiences with commodity-linked issues.

Introduction

These kinds of bond issues are by no means a novelty. The first known commodity bond, which is the most common form of commodity-linked financing, was issued by the Confederate States of America in 1863 (see Fall, 1986). The Confederates were fighting a costly war against the United States of America; their principal asset was cotton and, for that reason, they decided to issue a bond whose payoff would be linked to the price of cotton. Commodity bonds may also be linked to commodities other than the traditional primary ones. In 1945, for example, the French government's Caisse Nationale d'Energie issued a bond indexed on the price of electricity to pay for the nationalization of utilities. Investors were paid a 3 percent coupon and additional income from a fund that comprised 10 percent of the gross utility revenues in France.

As stated earlier, commodity bonds may be of two kinds: forward (often called commodity-indexed or convertible bonds) and option (often called commodity warrant bonds). For example, a conventional

US$1,000 10 percent coupon bond would make annual payments of US$100, while a similar oil bond of a forward type would, for instance, make coupon payments equal to the current monetary value of 5 barrels of Brendt oil. The payoffs to these bonds reveal that they are similar to a conventional bond and a set of forward contracts. Each coupon payment is analogous to a forward contract; however, there is one major difference. In a forward contract, the agreement is that the monetary settlement will take place at maturity. In a commodity bond, the investor who holds the long side has already fulfilled his obligation by buying the bond. Forward contracts are negotiated between two parties and are not always easily traded.

In a commodity bond of the option type, one or several call or put options are attached to the coupon or principal payments. In this case, the investor receives the US$1,000 face value and, in addition, has the option of buying or selling a predetermined quantity of oil at a predetermined price. Because these bonds include an option feature that has a market value, the coupon rate is generally lower than it would have been for a conventional bond. Thus, the advantage to the issuer of the option type is lower interest payments, with a tradeoff of sharing any appreciation in the price of the commodity by writing a call option on the commodity.

Issuers of commodity bonds are typically governments or corporations that have ready access to the underlying commodity and that seek a better hedge of their liabilities with their assets. The advantage to the investor is the ability to take a liquid and divisible position in a commodity, thus benefiting from a price hike (or fall) yet receiving a guaranteed minimum return on the investment (through the fixed coupon payments). Commodity bonds of both the option and forward type allow the holder to take a long-term commodity position. Thus, it would seem that commodity bonds would be popular with investors and issuers when commodity prices are expected to change significantly in either direction.

The proliferation of commodity bonds linked to precious metals (gold and silver) and to oil in recent years can be attributed to their image as an inflation hedge, their storability, and the natural position of several commercial banks in these markets. Uncertainty as to which U.S. agency—the Commodity Futures Trading Commission (CFTC) or the Securities and Exchange Commission (SEC)—should regulate these issues has caused most of the commodity-linked financings to take place in the Euromarkets. Since the October 1987 crash, Euromarket activity has subsided. At present, most commodity-linked financings are placed in the private markets. Australian and Canadian banks have become very active in these markets because of the importance of commodities to the Australian and Canadian economies. Data on private placements are scarce, but recent reports indicate that commodity-linked financings amount on an average of US$0.3 billion monthly.[1]

It is noteworthy that commodity-linked financing has taken forms other than those of the forward or option-type bonds. Some of these forms include those listed below.

Commodity-Indexed Certificates of Deposit

A bank-issued certificate of deposit (CD) typically pays interest to a depositor based on a percentage of the rise or decline in the price of a commodity or the value of an index during a specified period of time. The maturity, denomination, and manner in which interest is calculated on an indexed CD can vary substantially, and these differences reflect the disparate needs of savers.[2] In the United States, regulatory problems caused the abortion of gold CD issues by banks on the East and West Coasts in 1987. (See, for example, the Wells Fargo CD offering of September 1987.) In other countries, however, and, in particular, in Hong Kong, bear and bull gold CDs are available. (See, for example, the Banque Indosuez issue of February 1988.)

Commodity Variable-Rate Loans

A commodity variable-rate loan is made at an interest rate that is indexed to or correlates with an accepted benchmark of current market rates. The borrower's interest payments are adjusted at specified dates to reflect subsequent interest rate fluctuations. Such loans may have minimum or maximum rates set at the time of origination. Variable interest payments may be indexed to the value of a commodity produced by a borrower (see bullion loans below).

Gold Repos

Gold repos refers to an entity with excess gold that borrows cash from a bank for a specified period. Gold is used as collateral for the loan and is later repurchased by the borrower at a margin above a specified interest rate, but less than the cost of carrying gold during the relevant period. Thus, an entity with excess gold is able to meet a short-term funding requirement, and the bank makes a fully collateralized short-term loan at a rate higher than the market interest rate.

Bullion Loans

A bank may extend financing to a mining company indexed to bullion prices. The producer can use this comparatively low-cost financing to meet its working capital needs and deliver bullion (or the cash value thereof) to satisfy the loan repayment obligation.

Swaps

Swaps are privately negotiated transactions in which two parties, directly or through an intermediary bank, agree to exchange a series of payments calculated on different bases: fixed-rate interest payments for floating-rate payments, one type of floating-rate payment for another type of floating-rate payment, dollar-denominated payments for nondollar-denominated payments, fixed for floating commodity price payments, or payments tied to the price of one index for payments tied to the price of another. An exchange is arranged between two counterparties with complementary needs, and the payments due on the specified dates are netted. Swap transactions have been structured in innumerable forms and variations.[3]

Caps, Floors, and Collars

Caps and floors on commodity prices or other financial instruments are similar to swap transactions, except that the commodity price is fixed at a maximum (cap) or a minimum (floor). The seller of a cap agrees to pay the buyer the price differential between the capped and a floating price, with respect to a specified notional amount, in exchange for the payment of a fee. The seller of a floor agrees to pay the buyer the price differential between the floor and the floating price, with respect to a specified notional amount, in exchange for the payment of a fee. A collar is a transaction in which the purchaser of a cap simultaneously sells a floor to the seller of the cap, thereby defraying the cost of the cap.

Swaps, caps, floors, and collars are not financing instruments per se. Their hedging properties, however, have made their use increasingly important in commodity financing. As previously noted, in 1988, commodity financing relied more heavily on the types of financial instruments described above than on the more traditional Eurobond types. The following sections discuss particular experiences with gold, silver, oil, and other commodity-specific issues.

Gold-Linked Financing

Gold-linked financing has been the most widespread among forms of commodity-linked financing. The forward (or indexed) type and the option (or warrant) type have been the most typical forms of gold-linked financing. One of the best-known cases of gold bonds was that of the Giscard bond. In 1973, the French government appealed to investors with a gold-indexed bond issue. The "Giscard," as this bond is commonly referred to—named after the then-French finance minister (and later president) Valery Giscard d'Estaing—carried a 7 percent coupon rate and a redemption value indexed to the price of a 1 kilogram gold bar. The French government raised 6.5 billion French francs (FFr) with these bonds. The issue contained a clause under which interest and principal payments would be linked to gold if the French franc lost its parity with gold. With the floating of the French franc and the gold price since 1978, the safeguard clause was triggered, and, in 1980, the French government had to pay bondholders an exceptional FFr 393 in interest payments per bond—not the FFr 70 originally anticipated. The "Giscards," which were selling at par in 1977, increased in value by more than FFr 7,000 by the time they were redeemed in January 1988 at (an approximate) price of FFr 8,910.

Although in the case of "Giscards," only the principal was indexed directly to the gold price, other bonds issued since that time have linked interest and principal to gold prices. Such was the case with the issue by the Refinement International Company, a U.S. company, whose activities include the reclamation and refining of precious metals, the trading and financing of precious and other metals, and the manufacturing of precious metals' reclamation equipment. In January 1981, the company issued a 3.29 percent gold-indexed bond due in February 1996. In aggregate, the amount of principal was equal to the market price of 100,000 ounces of gold. Under the terms of issue, interest payments are made annually, and the interest and principal payments can be made in dollar terms or in gold terms on the basis of 10-day average market prices. Payments in gold are made in Zurich or in London.

Another version of a gold-linked security was issued in January 1981 by Echo Bay Mines Ltd., a subsidiary then of IU International Corporation. The company issued 1.55 million preferred voting shares of a particular type. Each of these shares gave the holder the right to a fixed US$3 annual dividend and 4 gold call warrants. Each warrant gave the holder the right to buy 0.0706 ounces of gold from Echo Bay at a price of US$595 per ounce. The four warrants were exercisable on different dates. The first was exercisable on January 31, 1986, the second on January 31, 1987, the third on January 31, 1988, and the fourth on January 31, 1989. All four warrants were able to be stripped from the preferred share and could be sold to a third party by December 30, 1983. These special preferred shares were offered at US$50 each. The issuers in their calculations valued the preferred share rights at US$25 and the warrants at US$25. Although this offering was not a bond, the preferred share resembles a perpetuity and can thus be treated as a special type of bond. The holder has the option to exercise the warrant and receive the physical quantity or choose under certain conditions to receive the difference between the actual price and the strike price, allowing for service and other fees. The physical exercise of the warrants was also linked to the completion of their Lupin Gold project.

Tables 2-1 and 2-2 show the gold bond issues of both the option type and the forward type made during the period from September 1986 to December 1988. These tables are by no means exhaustive. At present, there is no official source that regularly monitors these issues.[4] Gold loans and other types of gold-linked financing are not included.

A comparison of these gold-linked commodity bonds shows that there were more (approximately four times as many) bonds of the option type than of the forward type and that the preferred currency of the bonds of the option type was Swiss francs rather than U.S. dollars, although the opposite was true for the bonds of the convertible type. Some experimentation with the Canadian dollar and the European Currency Unit (ECU) also seems to have taken place. Gold warrants varied in length. Most were of two-year duration, but others extended to five years. Often the exercise of the warrants was earlier than the maturity of the bond. Most warrant-type bond issuers were banks or international corporations in the manufacturing business. Most forward-type bond issuers were corporations in the gold business. Two sovereign governments were among the recent issuers: Denmark and Belgium. The unrelated nature of most issuers to the gold business indicates that their aim was to raise funds at a lesser cost than otherwise possible by taking advantage of arbitrage possibilities in the longer-term side of the gold warrant market.

Tables 2-1 and 2-2 also show that the coverage with warrants was less than 50 percent in most cases and that the implied volatility at issue was close to historic levels in late 1986, but substantially higher thereafter. The strike price of the warrants was designed in such a way that the spot price would have the investor recover the option premium. In only two cases did bonds of the option-type include puts. Several bonds of the forward-type offered not only conversions into gold, but also provided additional kickers such as gold options or conversion into shares. The bonds of the forward-type are usually of a longer maturity than those of the option-type. The Pegassus issue is of a 10-year maturity, while most others are close to five years. The premium of the conversion price over the spot price varies between 20 percent and 50 percent.

As previously noted, the amount and size of gold loans has increased substantially since 1986. In the years 1984 through 1986, the median loan was probably about 30,000 ounces, while in 1987 and 1988, the median size increased to 70,000 ounces. In 1987, the largest loan was 100,000 ounces. In 1988, the issue for the refinancing of the Newmont mine was 1 million ounces, and there have been several other large loans, including those for Bond International Gold and Placer Dome. Lack of reliable information makes it difficult to review gold lending. It is

Table 2-1 *Gold Warrant Issues, 1986–88*

Issue date	Issue (lead manager)	Host bond	Warrant	Exercise price and period	Premium issue level	Implied volume at issue (percent)	Strike premium[a] (percent)	All-in premium[b] (percent)	Coverage ratio (percent)	Spot US$/oz
9/12/86	American Barrick Resources (Merrill Lynch Canada)	—	4 m Wrts each to buy 0.02 oz gold	US$9.20/0.02 oz (US$460/oz) 4 years (9/12/86–9/25/90)	US$1.50/0.02 oz (US$75/oz)	15	7	24	—	430
9/27/86	Echo Bay Mines Ltd. (Credit Suisse)	Sfr 110 m due 10/29/96 CPN: 3.875% Host bond and Wrt issued at 100	To each bond of Sfr 5,000 is 1 Wrt, exercisable into 6 oz of/or dollar equivalent of gold	US$560 5 years approx. (11/30/86–9/30/91)	Sfr 542/Wrt (Sfr 90 3/8/oz) (US$54/oz) (US$90.73/oz) (Spot FX = Sfr 1.6595/US$)	15	30	42	86	431
10/11/86	Standard Oil Co. (Morgan Guaranty)	Sfr 150 m due 11/6/93 CPN: 3.125% Host bond and Wrt issued at 100	To each bond of Sfr 5,000 is attached 1 Wrt, entitling the holder to purchase 3.3 oz of gold or receive the difference between spot price of gold and exercise price	US$565.20 4 years (11/6/87–11/6/91)	Sfr 500/Wrt (Sfr 151/5/oz) (US$90.73/oz) (Spot FX = Sfr 1.67/US$)	28	30	50	48	435

(Table continues on the following page.)

Table 2-1 (continued)

Issue date	Issue (lead manager)	Host bond	Warrant	Exercise price and period	Premium issue level	Implied volume at issue (percent)	Strike premium[a] (percent)	All-in premium[b] (percent)	Coverage ratio (percent)	Spot US$/oz
2/25/87	Credit Suisse (Credit Suisse, Zurich)	Sfr 200 m due 2/20/97 CPN: 2.875% Host bond and Wrt issued at 100	To each bond of Sfr 4,000 are attached 10 Wrts, allowing together the purchase of 100g of fine gold (1 oz = 31.1035g)	US$565.20 (US$467.98 oz) 3 years (3/20/87–3/20/90)	Sfr 500/Wrt (Sfr 162/oz) (US$105.3/oz) (Spot FX = Sfr1.5385/US$)	42	15	40.3	50.2	407
3/3/87	Citibank (Citibank NA, Zurich)	—	10,000 Wrts exercisable into 10 oz of fine gold or equiv. cash amount	US$430/oz 2 years (4/16/87–4/16/89)	Sfr 1,050/Wrt (Sfr 105/oz) (US$68.2/oz) (Spot FX = Sfr1.5395/US$)	25	6½	23.5	—	403
3/5/87	Financiere Credit Suisse First Boston (Credit Suisse)	Sfr 100 m due 3/30/97 CPN: 3.25% Host bond and Wrt issued at 100	To each bond of Sfr 5,000 are attached 10 Wrts, allowing purchase of 100g of fine gold (1 oz = 31.1035g)	Sfr 2.335/100g (US$465.7/oz) 3 years (3/30/87–3/30/90)	Sfr 540/10 Wrt (Sfr 167.95/oz) (US$107.7/oz) (Spot FX = Sfr1.56/US$)	40	13	43	41	412

Date	Issuer (Lead)	Terms	Exercise	Warrant / FX						Page
3/5/87	Citibank (Citibank NA, Zurich)	10,000 Wrts, each exercisable into 10 oz of fine gold or equivalent cash	US$420/oz 15 months (4/22/87–10/3/88)	Sfr 950/Wrt (Sfr 95/oz) (US$60.9/oz) (Spot FX = Sfr1.56/US$)	24	2	18	—		412
3/6/87	Banque Indosuez (Goldman Sachs)	15,000 Wrts, each entitling holder to buy 10 oz gold	US$410/oz 2 years (4/16/87–4/16/89)	Sfr 1.380/Wrt (Sfr 138/oz) (Spot FX = Sfr 1.55/US$)	29	0.861	21.7	—		406
3/18/87	Morgan Guaranty Trust (MG, AG, Switzer-land)	12,000 Wrts, each to bring 5 oz of fine gold	US$425/oz 4¼ years (4/30/87–7/31/91)	Sfr 995/Wrt (Sfr 191/oz) (US$124.6/oz) (Spot FX = Sfr 1.5335/US$)	26.5	4.41	35	—		407
3/25/87	Electricite de France (Credit Suisse Zurich)	Sfr 100m due 4/20/95 CPN: 3.375% Host bond and Wrt issued at 100	To each note of Sfr 50,000 are attached 15 gold Wrts issued by Credit Suisse, each exercisable into 50g of fine gold	Sfr 2.350/100g (US$481/oz) 3 years (4/30/87–4/04/90)	Sfr 4.489/15 Wrt (Sfr 186/oz) (US$122.5/oz) (Spot FX = Sfr1.5195/US$)	45	15	44.4	28.6		418
4/9/87	Kingdom of Belgium (Credit Suisse Zurich)	Sfr 100m due 4/20/94 CPN: 3.375% Host bond and Wrt issued at 100	To each note of Sfr 50,000 are attached 15 gold Wrts, each exercisable into 50g of fine gold	Sfr 3.666/15 Wrt (Sfr 152/oz) (US$101.5/oz) (Spot FX = Sfr1.4972/US$)	39	19	43	30.8		427

(Table continues on the following page.)

Table 2-1 (continued)

Issue date	Issue (lead manager)	Host bond	Warrant	Exercise price and period	Premium issue level	Implied volume at issue (percent)	Strike premium[a] (percent)	All-in premium[b] (percent)	Coverage ratio (percent)	Spot US$/oz
4/14/87	Citibank NA (Citicorp)	—	20,000 Wrts each to bring 5 oz of fine gold	US$440/oz 21 months (5/4/87–2/4/89)	Sfr 610/Wrt (Sfr 122/oz) (US$82/oz) (Spot FX = Sfr 1.4878/US$)	25	—	18.5	—	444
4/15/87	Saint-Gobain (Salomon Bros.)	ECU 75m due 5/6/92 CPN: 4.5% Host bond and Wrt issued at 100	To each bond of ECU 1,000 is attached a gold Wrt, exercisable into 1 oz of fine gold	US$490/oz 3 years (5/6/87–5/6/90)	US$135/Wrt (Spot FX = US$1.1154/ECU)	39.5	10	41	49.5	444
4/15/87	BNP (CSFB)	US$100m due 5/13/92 CPN: zero Host bond and Wrt issued at 80	To each bond of US$1,000 is attached 1 Wrt to buy 1 oz of gold	US$496/oz 3 years (5/13/87–4/16/90)	US$150/oz	45	12	45.5	44.4	444
4/16/87	Hoffman La Roche (Credit Suisse)	Sfr 250m due 9/30/90 CPN: zero Host bond and Wrt issued at 80.5	To each bond of Sfr 5,000 are attached 10 Wrts, exercisable into 100g of fine gold	Sfr 2.510/100g (US$522.2/oz) 3½ years (5/15/87–9/30/90)	Sfr 238.5/oz (US$158.5/oz) (Spot FX = Sfr 1.495/US$)	52	21.7	55	42.2	429

Date	Issuer (Lead)	Bond	Warrant terms	Exercise price	Reference					Page
4/16/87	Kingdom of Belgium (Credit Suisse)	Sfr 50m due 4/20/92 CPN: 3% Host bond and Wrt issued at 100	To each note of Sfr 50,000 are attached 15 gold Wrts, each exercisable into 50g	Sfr 2.520/100g (US$524.3/oz) 3 years (4/20/87–4/20/90)	Sfr 472/100g = 147/oz (US$98.3/oz) (Spot FX = Sfr 1.495/US$)	34	16.7	38.5	32.4	449
5/14/87	Aegon (Citicorp)	Sfr 100m due 6/16/92 CPN: 2.5% Host bond and Wrt issued at 100	To each bond of Sfr 50,000 are attached 5 Wrts, each exercisable into 5 oz	US$500/oz 23 months (6/17/87–5/15/89)	US$113/oz	37	7.8	32	36.5	464
5/20/87	Eastman Kodak & Co. (UBS)	US$ 130m due 6/25/90 CPN: 9% IP: 113.175 (cum Wrts) 101.375 (ex Wrts)	To each bond of US$5,000 are attached 5 Wrts, each exercisable into 1 oz	US$470/oz 23 months (6/25/87–5/19/89)	US$118/oz	32	—	25	47.06	470
5/21/87	Eksportfinans (UBS)	US$100m due 6/22/90 CPN: 9% IP:113.18 (cum Wrts) 101.18 (ex Wrts)	To each bond of US$5,000 are attached 5 Wrts, each exercisable into 1 oz	US$475/oz 23 months (6/23/87–5/22/89)	US$120/oz	32	—	25	47.5	476

(Table continues on the following page.)

Table 2-1 (continued)

Issue date	Issue (lead manager)	Host bond	Warrant	Exercise price and period	Premium issue level	Implied volume at issue (per cent)	Strike premium[a] (per cent)	All-in premium[b] (per cent)	Coverage ratio (percent)	Spot US$/oz
5/21/87	General Motors Canada (Citicorp)	Sfr 120m due 6/30/92 CPN: 2.750% Host bond and Wrt issued at 100	To each bond of Sfr 50,000 are attached 5 Wrts, each exercisable into 5 oz	US$510/oz 17 months	US$99/oz	38	8.1	29	37.23	472
5/21/87	UBS (UBS)	Sfr 200m due 6/15/97 CPN: 3¼% Host bond and Wrts issued at 100	To each bond of Sfr 5,000 are attached 10 Wrts, together exercisable into 100g of fine gold	Sfr 2.575/100g (Sfr 801/oz) (US$548/oz) 3 years (6/15/87–6/15/90)	Sfr 495/10 Wrts (Sfr 154/oz) (US$105/oz) (Spot FX = 1.4600)	34	16	38	44.3	472
5/29/87	Christiania Bank (Gutzwiller)	Sfr 50m due 7/8/94 CPN: 2½% Host bond and Wrts issued at 100	To each bond of Sfr 5,000 are attached 3 call and 4 put Wrts on difference London fixing and strike per 1 oz fine gold	Call: strike = US$490 18 months (until 11/30/88) Put: strike = US$420 3 years (until 5/31/90)	Call: US$83.2/oz Put: US$46.1/oz (Spot FX = 1.4600 Sfr/US$)	Call: 34 Put: 31¾	—	Call: 27 Put: 17	Call: 27.1 Put: 36.1	451.25

6/30/87	DNC (Gutzwiller)	Sfr 50m due 6/20/94 CPN: 2½% Host bond and Wrts issued at 100	To each bond of Sfr 5,000 are attached 3 call and 4 put Wrts on difference London fixing and strike per 10 oz fine gold	Call: strike = US$440 18 months Put: strike = US$410 3 years	Call: US$83.2/oz Put: US$41.7/oz (Spot FX = 1.5010 Sfr/US$)	Call: 34 Put: 31½	—	Call: 26 Put: 19	Call: 27.3 Put: 36.4	455.10
7/25/87	Citibank NA (Citicorp)	—	10,000 naked gold warrants, each Wrt allows the holder to purchase 10 oz of fine gold	US$420/oz (until 10/11/88)	Sfr 1.490/Wrt (US$963.89/Wrt) (US$96.38/oz) (Spot FX = 1.5495 Sfr/US$)	32	—	13	—	457
8/4/87	Rhone Poulenc (Shearson Lehman)	Sfr 100m due 9/8/95 CPN: 2% Host bond and Wrts issued at 100	To each bond of Sfr 5,000 is attached 1 Wrt, exercisable into 4.2 oz of gold (public issue)	US$475/oz (9/11/87–5/22/89)	Sfr 897.7/Wrt (Sfr 213.7/oz) (US$137.7/oz) (Spot FX = 1.5523 Sfr/US$)	41	—	29	61	475
8/6/87	Olivetti (UBS, SBC, Shearson Lehman)	Sfr 100m due 9/21/96 CPN: 2% Host bond and Wrts issued at 100	To each bond of Sfr 5,000 is attached 1 Wrt, exercisable into 4.6 oz of gold (public issue)	US$465/oz (until 5/22/89)	Sfr 988.3/Wrt (Sfr 214.85/oz) (US$137.77/oz) (Spot FX = 1.5595 Sfr/US$)	44	—	28.5	67	469

(Table continues on the following page.)

Table 2-1 (continued)

Issue date	Issue (lead manager)	Host bond	Warrant	Exercise price and period	Premium issue level	Implied volume at issue (per-cent)	Strike premium[a] (per-cent)	All-in premium[b] (per-cent)	Coverage ratio (percent)	Spot US$/oz
8/11/87[c]	SEK (Warburg Soditic)	Sfr 100m due 10/15/94 CPN: 2⅜% Host bond and Wrts issued at 100; 20% amortization yearly from 1990–94	To each bond of Sfr 5,000 is attached 1 Wrt, exercisable into 2.6 oz of gold (public issue: fees 1⅞%)	US$460/oz 2 years	Sfr 437.1/Wrt (Sfr 174.9/oz) (US$111.34/oz) (Spot FX = 1.5705 Sfr/US$)	29.5	—	23.4	42	463
9/22/87	FBDB (Dominion Securities)	C$50m due 11/4/91 CPN: 10¼% Host bond and Wrts issued at 113½	To each bond of C$5,000 are attached 5 Wrts, each one exercisable into 1 oz of gold (public issue)	US$463.15/oz 2 years (until 9/21/89)	C$140.79/Wrt (US$106.98/oz)	26.5	—	23.2	61	463

24

| 9/23/87 | ATT (UBS) | US$100m due 10/22/90 CPN: 9¼% Host bond and Wrts issued at 112¾ | To each bond of US$5,000 are attached 5 Wrts, each one exercisable into 1 oz of gold (public issue: fees 1⅜%) | US$463/oz 2 years (10/22/87–9/21/89) | US$120/oz | 35 | — | 26.2 | 46 | 462 |

— Not available.

m = million.

a. Defined as strike price/spot price.

b. Defined as (exercise price + option premium)/spot price of gold. The spot price of gold has to increase by this percentage from its current level for the investor to break even (i.e., recover the option premium).

c. This deal was pulled and replaced by a series of zero coupon tranches.

Source: Goldman Sachs, London, February 1988.

25

Table 2-2 Gold Indexed and Convertible Issues

Issue date	Issuer (lead manager)	Amount (denoms)	Issue price	Coupon (percent)	Maturity	Conversion details	Conversion price	Comments
1/16/73	French government	FFr 6.5 m (FFr 1,000)	100	7	1/16/88	—	—	Redemption and coupon are indexed to: (1) The price of 1 kg of gold in Paris on issue date, i.e., FFr 10.483 (2) The average price of 1 kg of gold for the 30 business days before January 1. Coupon (per bond) = (70/10,483) × (2) Redemption (per bond) = (1,000/10,483) × (2)
10/4/86	American Barrick Resources (Banque Paribas)	US$50 m	100	5¼	10/31/91	Into gold from 10/31/91	$530/oz	Redemption price = 111½
1/24/87	Barrick Resources guaranteed by American Barrick Resources (Banque Paribas)	US$50 m	100	2	2/29/92	Into gold or US$ equivalent with conversion price reducing by $16 per 100g per year commencing 2/26/89 (i.e. about $5/oz)	$406.84/oz	—

Issuer (Lead manager)	Amount	Price	Coupon	Maturity	Issue date	Conversion	Conversion terms	Redemption
Pegasus Gold Corp. (Banque Gutzwiller)	Sfr 60 m (Sfr 5,000)	100	5¾	10/10/96	9/19/86	(1) Into shares: until 9/19/96 (2) Into cash equivalent of gold during last three years of maturity	(1) Into shares: at $9.607/share at FX (Sfr 1.6576/US$) corresponding to 314 shares/bond (Premium = 10.069%) (2) Into gold: to buy 4.89 oz of fine gold/bond at $617.25/oz (Premium = 50%)	—
Kingdom of Denmark (Societe Generale)	US$120 m Two tranches: Bull-$60 m Bear-$60 m	100⅛	3	10/20/93		—	—	Redemption linked to price of gold: Bull = Par × 1.158 Price of gold at maturity/ Price of gold at issue ($426.5/oz) Bear = Par × 2.78–1.158 Price of gold at maturity/Price of gold at issue ($426.5/oz)

(Table continues on the following page.)

Table 2-2 (continued)

Issue date	Issuer (lead manager)	Amount (denoms)	Issue price	Coupon (percent)	Maturity	Conversion details	Conversion price	Comments
4/16/87	International Corona Resources (Banque Paribas)	US$50,001,107 of bonds convertible into gold with attached gold call warrants	100	3⅛	5/12/92	(1) Convertible into gold from 5/15/88 to 5/15/92 (2) 1 Wrt is attached to each bond—a 3-year call on gold	(1) Convertible into gold at $16.91/g (=$526.02/oz—20% premium of spot) (2) Call on gold at $17.62/g (=$547.94/oz—25% premium of spot)	—
5/5/87	Hycroft (Banque Gutzwiller)	US$12.152 m minimum to 17.361 m maximum	105	5	5/28/92	(1) Conversion period: 12/1/87 to maturity: changeable for 100g gold bullion or (2) For amount equal to current market value of 100g gold bullion	(1) Conversion price = $540/oz (20% over premium over spot gold)	—

— Not available. m = million.
Source: Goldman Sachs, London, February 1988.

estimated, however, that since 1986, there have been loans totaling approximately 7 million ounces, some 50 percent of which have been arranged since October 1987. Gold loans are used primarily to fund mine developments and expansion. Some loans, however, have been used to refinance corporate debt. The unresponsiveness of the equity markets to the hedging needs of the mining community and the proliferation of know-how in the pricing of these loans have made them increasingly acceptable to the industry.

The average length of gold loans has also increased in the past few years. This resulted from the needs of the mining industry. Capital costs increased with the exploitation of deeper or lower quality ores, and some exogenous factors (such as the introduction of income taxes for gold mining in Australia) affected the rate of return of the projects. The loan terms have lengthened, but they remain limited by the life of a borrower's ore reserves. The increasing size of loans has led to some changes in lending and pricing practices. The practice of capping interest rates on gold loans has all but disappeared. Increasing competition and fluctuating borrowing costs have reduced lender's margins, making stable interest rates a matter of history. As the size of loans has increased, lenders have also begun to spread risks by syndicating loans to other lenders. The move away from single-lender loans is moving gold lending toward a cost-plus-margin basis (analogous to currency lending).

A variety of references are in use, including agent bank base rate, lead bank group reference rate, and tender panel and benchmark reference rate. A COMEX-reference borrowing rate is determined by subtracting a futures market contago from a relevant London interbank offered rate (LIBOR). The contago may reflect a spot-to-forward or a forward-to-forward contango. The LIBOR rate used has a term similar to that of the longest futures contract used in the contango calculation. The volatility of gold borrowing rates and average rates have increased recently. Scarce physical stocks and other factors have often caused rates to reach high levels. Sourcing of gold for Japan's Hirohito coin and the Taiwanese Central Bank gold purchases have depleted exchange stocks, leading to temporary increases in borrowing rates. There is a general agreement among market participants that interest rate levels have increased between 0.5 percent and 0.75 percent during 1988.

Loan agreements now routinely contain provision for automatic conversion of debt to dollars in the event of a gold market disruption. As far as is known, there have been few defaults on gold loans. In November 1988, a small Australian producer, Solomon Pacific Resources NL, was reported to have fallen behind on its gold loan repayments, apparently due to higher-than-expected operating costs. In Canada, Pacific Trans-Ocean Resources reportedly ran into problems in meeting its loan obligations. The problems included higher-than-expected development costs, lower-than-expected head grades, and excessive dilution. These two incidents are isolated cases. The relatively small size of the companies and their relatively weak financial position are not typical of gold borrowers. It is noteworthy that several central banks of both developing and developed countries use their gold reserves for lending purposes. Their lending is driven primarily by their desire to derive income from an otherwise idle asset. Gold lending is still a very small part of total bank lending. Gold lenders are able to access gold to fund their commitments by taking deposits from central banks, from other market participants, and through swaps. Swaps, as previously noted, involve purchasing gold on a spot basis and reselling it forward to other market participants or through COMEX.

It is uncertain whether these gold-linked financings have affected the price of gold. Some analysts say that increased lending has caused prices to fall as the sale of metal has been brought forward in time, swamping markets. Others believe this is untrue because new production that otherwise would be sold into the market is instead now committed to loan repayments, thus putting an upward pressure on prices.

As the gold industry is rapidly turning to the exploitation of larger, deeper sulfide deposits and as consolidation in the industry seems to be leading to the formation of large mining groups, the market for gold loans will continue to mature, surpassing that of gold bonds of the warrant type. Most new gold projects have a production cost of US$200–US$225 per ounce and a financing cost of US$70–US$80 per ounce. With a 20 percent pretax investor return for such projects, the prospective investors' minimum break-even price should be about US$325–US$365 per ounce. Consequently, gold prices below US$400 per ounce would tend to discourage new investment and exploration, reducing the demand for gold loans. If average prices increase, more gold-linked financing could be expected. Independent of new investments, existing gold-related companies are increasingly expected to use hedging tools to reduce their risk-reward profile so that they can appeal to a wider, more risk-averse segment of the investment community.[5]

Silver-Linked Financing

The best-known silver-linked financings are those of the Sunshine Mining Company. The Sunshine Mining Company is the largest silver producer in the United States. With silver prices fluctuating between US$6 per ounce in 1979 to a peak of US$50 per ounce in January 1980 and back to US$33 per ounce in February 1980, the Sunshine Mining

Company decided to issue commodity bonds to try to hedge variations in working capital.

In 1980, the company raised US$25 million with the issue of 8½ percent silver-indexed bonds due April 15, 1995. The bonds make semiannual coupon payments, and the largest principal payments are US$1,000 or the market value of 50 ounces of silver. The bonds trade on the New York Stock Exchange. Under the terms of issue, the bonds can be redeemed on or after April 15, 1985 if the average silver price for 30 consecutive days is greater than US$40 per ounce. The company has the right to propose redemption of 70 percent of its original issue from 1982 and thereafter. The company is not restricted from the creation of senior indebtedness, but must maintain qualified reserves equal to or higher than 400 percent of the aggregate amount of silver required by all outstanding silver-backed and silver-related securities. The investors can take a position in the silver market while earning a good return from their investment, and the silver producer raises funds at a cost lower than otherwise would have been possible.

Sunshine Mining Corporation issued a second silver bond totaling US$40 million in April 1985 for April 2004 maturity. The coupon was 9¾ percent, and the principal is the greatest of callable US$1,000 or 58 ounces of silver. The issue has properties similar to the previous one. (See table 2-3.)

Contrary to the case with gold, the volume of silver loans is not significant. The most important reason for the lack of development of silver-linked financing is because silver prices have changed little since 1980, trading in the range of US$6–8 per ounce during that time. At these prices, silver producing companies do not invest in new projects. Operating costs of new ventures are in the US$4–5 per ounce range. When financing costs and a 20 percent pretax profit margin are added to these costs, there is little incentive for silver producers to undertake new ventures. As with gold, silver-linked financing would increase if silver prices increase substantially from their present level. In the absence of such price increases, investment activity will only focus on refinancing existing ventures and on hedging existing profit margins.

Crude-Oil-Linked Financing

Crude-oil-linked bonds and other forms of oil-linked financing began in the late 1970s after substantial petroleum price increases, but their use became popular only in recent years. Indeed, the Reagan administration considered seriously the issuing of bonds linked to oil to finance an increase in the U.S. strategic petroleum reserve in early 1981. Among the

Table 2-3 *Silver-Linked Issues, 1985–88*

Issue date	Issuer (lead manager)	Amount	Issue price	Coupon (percent)	Maturity	Indexation	Comment
April 1985	Sunshine Mining (Drexel Burnham Lambert)	US$40 m	100	9¾	4/15/2004	Each $1,000 bond is redeemed at maturity at the greater of $1,000 or the average market price of 58 oz of silver ("Indexed Principal Amount")	The bonds are redeemable in whole from 4/15/90 at the option of the company, at the IPA plus accrued interest, if the IPA is greater than or equal to $2,000 for a period of 30 consecutive calendar days

Source: Goldman Sachs, London, February 1988.

first known oil bond issues were those by the Mexican government. The "Petrobonds," as the Mexican oil bonds are known, were issued in bearer form by a trust fund set up by the National Financiere S.A. (NAFINSA). NAFINSA is a development bank owned by the Mexican government. The Petrobonds are listed on the Mexican Stock Exchange.

The objective in issuing these bonds was to entice back the money that fled the country following the 45 percent devaluation of the Mexican peso in 1976. The first issue took place in April 1977. Almost 2 billion pesos were raised, and the funds were used to finance Mexican oil development. The bonds had a maturity of three years and carried a coupon of 12.66 percent payable quarterly. The coupon was subject to a 21 percent Mexican withholding tax. After tax, the coupon netted approximately 10 percent. At maturity, the bondholder received the peso value of a pre-specified number of barrels of Mexican oil net of the nominal value of coupon receipts. The average oil export price for the 25 days preceding the maturity date was used for the calculation of the payment. Each barrel of Mexican oil per bond used in the calculation was worth 1,000 pesos at the time of the issue.

With this issue, the government was not only raising new money at low nominal cost, but also was hedging a part of its oil production. The investors in these bonds were participating in the possible upswing of oil prices. The Mexican government has made five successful issues of Petrobonds. The importance of oil for the development of the Mexican economy was also recognized by the International Monetary Fund (IMF) restructuring agreement of the mid-1980s, under which the U.S. government was committed to increasing the availability of financing to the Mexican economy when oil prices dropped below a certain benchmark and reducing U.S. credit availability when oil prices increased above another.

In 1981, Petro-Lewis Corporation, a Denver-based company in oil exploration and production raised US$20 million with oil-linked notes. The notes carried a 9 percent annual coupon rate, and they matured in five years. At maturity, the investors received the principal, its annual coupon, and an option. The option exercisable at maturity was based on average spot prices of several oil types. It was of the call variety and had a cap. By exercising this option, an investor could make at most an additional US$589 per bond. This kicker makes this type of bond attractive to investors. The borrower raises funds at lower cost than would otherwise have been possible, while foregoing some of the upside revenue potential from part of its oil assets.

A long-term call or put commodity option resembles a zero commodity-linked bond of the option type. In this case, the "conventional bond" share in the commodity bond is reduced to zero. Several of these

Table 2-4 Oil-Linked Issues, 1985–88

Issue date	Issuer (lead manager)	Host bond (debenture)	Warrant	Description	Comment
9/27/85	Phibro-Salomon Inc. (Salomon)	(naked issue)	(1) 16,000 call Wrts offered in four series of 4,000 per series, each Wrt to buy 1,000 U.S. barrels of WTI	A—exercisable on 5/13/86 at $28/bbl; AA—exercisable on 5/13/86 at $30/bbl; B—exercisable on 11/14/86 at $28/bbl; BB—exercisable on 11/14/86 at $30/bbl	Holder of warrants can choose between physical and net settlement. If net settlement, the following formulae apply: (1) Call net settlement = 3-day average call futures oil-price × 1,000 price (2) Put net settlement = put 3-day average price—futures oil × 1,000 price
			(2) 16,000 put Wrts offered in four series of 4,000 per series, each Wrt to sell 1,000	C—exercisable on 5/13/86 at $23/bbl; CC—exercisable on 5/13/86 at $21/bbl; D—exercisable on 11/14/86 at $23/bbl; DD—exercisable on 11/14/86 at $21/bbl	
6/16/86	Standard Oil Co. (Goldman Sachs)	CPN: 6.30% (s.a.) Amt: $300 m Denoms: $1,000 IP: 100% Mat: 6/15/2001	(1) Indexed Note 1 CPN: Zero Amt: $37.5 m Denoms: $1,000 IP: 100% Mat: 12/15/92	Redemption = $100 + (\text{WTI price} - 25) \times 170$[a]	Bonds issued in "units," each of which consisted of 8 debentures of $1,000 denoms, 1 oil indexed note 1 (due 1990), and 1 oil indexed note 2 (due 1990)

		(2) *Indexed Note 2* CPN: Zero Amt: $37.5 m Denoms: $1,000 IP: 100% Mat: 3/15/92		Redemption = 100 = (WTI price − 25) × 200[a]	—
					Private placement
7/8/87	Kredintbank (Goldman Sachs)	CPN: 3% (ann) Amt: Sfr 50 m Denoms: Sfr 50,000 IP: 100.5% Mat: 8/14/92	Attached to each Sfr 50,000 note are 2 Wrts, each to buy 250 U.S. barrels of WTI crude oil (American calls)	Exercise period: 2 years Exercise price: US$21/bbl	Private placement
7/8/87	Christiania Bank (Banque Gutzwiller)	CPN: 2⅝% (ann) Amt: Sfr 20 m Denoms: Sfr 5,000 IP: 100%	Attached to each Sfr 5,000 bond is 1 Wrt to buy 100 U.S. barrels of WTI crude oil (American calls)	Exercise period: 3 years Exercise price: US$23/bb1	Public issue that was pulled (i.e., never actually materialized)
7/12/87	Montedison Finance (Morgan Stanley)	CPN: 4⅞% (ann) Amt: Sfr 75 m Denoms: Sfr 5,000 and 100,000 IP: 122% Mat: 8/27/92	Attached to each Sfr 5,000 bonds are 7 Wrts, each to buy 20 U.S. barrels of WTI crude oil (American calls)	Exercise period: 3 years Exercise price: US$23.55/bbl	Public issue

— Not available.

a. There is a cap on the West Texas Intermediate (WTI) crude oil price of $40 per barrel.

Source: World Bank data.

long-term (more than a year) commodity options have been written in the last three to four years. Gold, silver, and oil products were not the only commodities for which long-term options were written. Well-known cases include nickel, copper, aluminum, and other metals. Unfortunately, because most of these contracts take place outside official exchanges, it is very difficult to have an accurate estimate of the liquidity of these markets. It is, nevertheless, well known that an increasing number of commercial and investment houses are willing to quote a price for creditworthy organizations. The increased use of these option instruments, particularly with oil, has also helped the development of the oil swap markets. These long-term oil options are used for hedging purposes. In 1985, for example, Phibro-Salomon Inc., a New-York-based investment and trading house, offered its clients 16,000 West Texas Intermediate (WTI) oil puts and as many calls with expiration dates of 8 and 14 months. In conjunction with a straight financing arrangement, long-term commodity options can compose the two parts of a commodity-linked financing. (As discussed later, however, there are important benefits to investors to have the two parts of a commodity-linked financing in one contract rather than in two.)

During the past three years, several oil bond issues took place. (See table 2-4.) Almost all were of the forward type. Because of the uncertainties of the regulatory environment, only one took place in U.S. financial markets. This was the Sohio Oil Company issue. Sohio, a major U.S. oil producer, decided to use this method to finance a common venture with BP and to hedge their oil assets. Sohio issued oil-indexed units (OIUs). The offer was composed of (1) US$300 million, 6.3 percent oil-indexed debentures (OIDs), due in 2001, priced at 747, and yielding 9.59 percent; (2) US$37.5 million detachable oil-indexed notes (OINs) due in 1990; and (3) US$37.5 million detachable OINs due in 1992. Each OIU consisted of nine OIDs, one 1990 OIN and one 1992 OIN. For the OINs, if the spot price of oil exceeds US$25 per barrel, the note holder gets the excess multiplied by 170 barrels for each 1990 note and the excess multiplied by 200 for each 1992 note—with the excess not to exceed US$15 per barrel. Therefore, the effective yield on each OIU varies from a low of 8.3 percent, if the oil price is below US$25, to a high of 13.9 percent when oil is US$40 per barrel. Each US$1,000 OIN is effectively a combination of a zero coupon bond priced at US$747 and an attached call option with an initial value of US$253. The option was coupled to the zero because the CFTC prohibits the existence of naked or securitized options with greater than 18 months' maturity, unless the security option is less than 50 percent of the value of the bond. The proposed 1989 CFTC ruling on hybrid instruments recommends a lower threshold percentage.

Oil bond issues are expected to increase sharply in the years to come.

The median cost of production of crude oil is still very low in comparison with the present prices of crude oil. Oil bonds can help finance the exploration and development of new projects or restructure the finances of existing oil companies.

Other Commodity-Linked Issues

There have also been commodity-linked financings in nickel, copper, zinc, and other commodities. The motivations for these issues were multiple. The most often quoted reasons, however, were to raise funds at low nominal cost and to hedge part of production from commodity price risks.

Inco, the world's most important nickel producer and an important producer of copper, silver, cobalt, and platinum, issued a Can$90 million bond indexed to nickel or copper prices in 1984. The issue came with a 10 percent coupon. The bonds mature in 1991. The bondholders have the privilege of either requesting the principal at par or to be paid the monetary equivalent of prefixed quantities of nickel or copper. The exchange right of the investors could have been exercised prior to 1987 if the nickel London Metal Exchange (LME) cash price exceeded US$2.90 per pound or the copper (LME cash) price exceeded US$0.80 per pound. Inco had the option to repay in cash or in common shares. In 1984, Inco was experiencing financial difficulties. With this issue, the company was able to raise funds at a cost substantially below what it would have had to pay otherwise.

In 1988, Inco considered the issue of a second nickel bond. Its reason for doing so this time was to reduce its exposure to nickel price fluctuations. In 1988, nickel prices had reached unprecedented levels; the company was in a strong financial position and did not need to borrow additional funds. Inco found it more appropriate, however, to hedge its nickel price risks through long-term contracts with its major customers—thereby locking 25 percent of its production during the next three years to prices substantially higher than its average costs.

In 1987, Cominco Ltd., an important Canadian mining company in the copper and zinc business, raised US$54 million for the financing of its investment program through the sale of preferred shares and commodity-indexed common share purchase warrants (CIS). Each CIS provides the holder with the right to exchange the warrant on or before August 1992 for a number of common shares of the corporation to be determined based on the average market price of zinc or copper and on the average market price of common shares on the date of the exercise. Each unit was offered at US$18, of which US$11.75 was allocated for the preferred shares and US$6.25 for each warrant.

In 1988, Magma, the largest copper producer in the United States, issued an even more innovative structure of notes linked to copper prices. The US$200 million issue, due in 1998, linked interest payments to copper prices. The quarterly interest payments were paying 18 percent at the time of the issue. The copper-indexed interest rate will range from 21 percent per annum at average copper prices of US$2 per pound and above to 12 percent per annum at average copper prices at US$0.80 per pound and below. The proceeds of the offering were used to restructure the liabilities of the company. The indexing of the interest payments to copper prices makes this issue one of the best examples of corporate balance sheet refinancing for risk management purposes. With this issue, Magma succeeds in linking expenses with revenues and, in the process, assuring stability in profitability and net worth. The nominal cost of financing makes this a high yield offering. Institutional and other investors in the high yield market were attracted to this issue.

Several commodity-linked issues have taken place in developing countries. Citibank is reported to have underwritten a small loan linked to palm oil prices in Malaysia. Metallgesellschaft is reported to have financed its copper investments in Papua New Guinea with copper-linked financing. Lack of transparency in privately arranged financings makes it very difficult to determine an accurate number and amount of commodity-linked financings in both developing and developed countries. Confidential reports from major banking and commodity trading houses, however, do, indicate extensive use of these methods for financing or refinancing investment programs in the commodities industries.

Notes

1. One billion equals one thousand million. See proceedings from the Fifth Mineral Economics Symposium, 1989, Toronto, Canada.

2. A version of this CD type—the College Sure CD—provides a return on maturity based on a multiple of the average cost of a college education to enable depositors to cover the costs of their children's college education.

3. Swaps are written on forward and amortizing bases and may include various option-like features. The latter are referred to as swap options or "swaptions." Swaps can also be participating, extendable, or callable and have drawdown provisions.

4. Goldman Sachs has kindly provided us with these tables.

5. See Woodward (1989) and Stone (1989).

3

The Demand for Commodity Bonds

Moctar A. Fall

One of the most important models in finance theory, the Sharpe-Lintner Capital Asset Pricing Model (CAPM), is based on a single-period model with very restrictive assumptions (Sharpe, 1964). Although the model has been widely criticized and widely tested by the academic community, it is still extensively used in the nonacademic world. This chapter derives the demand functions for commodity bonds using a continuous-time intertemporal model similar to the one derived by Merton (1971, 1973). The model applies a dynamic programming technique to the consumption-portfolio problem for a household whose income is generated by capital gains on investments in tradable assets. The derivations are done in nominal terms. The chapter begins with a one-consumption good version of this model and continues with a multigood extension.

The One-Consumption Good Case

Assumptions

The general assumptions retained for this analysis are similar to the ones made in Merton (1973a). Households are assumed to behave as price takers in a perfectly competitive market, and trading always takes place at equilibrium prices. Households can buy and sell as much of an asset as they want at market prices and may short-sell any asset with full use of the proceeds. It is further assumed that households hold wealth in the form of risky assets and an instantaneously riskless asset for which the borrowing and lending rates are equal. All assets are assumed to be perfectly divisible and have limited liability. Households can trade continuously and face no transaction costs or taxes. Finally, asset prices are assumed to be stationary and log-normally distributed.

Most of the assumptions made are the standard assumptions required to make a perfect market. These have been widely discussed in the finance literature and are mainly retained for the sake of simplicity, while doing no damage to the analysis. Nevertheless, Fama argues in Cootner (1964) that stock and commodity price changes follow a stable Paretian distribution with infinite second moments. It is important to note, however, that nothing has been said about the homogeneity of households' expectations, as is required in the derivation of the CAPM and similar models.

Asset Returns

In this section, there is a single consumption good, the commodity whose price is assumed to be generated by an Ito process:

$$(3\text{-}1) \qquad \frac{dP_1}{P_1} = \alpha_1 dt + \sigma_1 dz_1$$

where α_1 is the expected percentage change in the commodity's price per unit time and σ_1 is the instantaneous variance per unit time. The instantaneously riskless rate of interest is assumed to follow the following differential equation:

$$(3\text{-}2) \qquad dr = \alpha_r dt + \sigma_r dz_r$$

Each individual can hold three assets in the portfolio: a commodity bond, equity, and a default-free bond. The value of the commodity bond depends only on the price of the commodity, the rate of interest, and time until maturity.

$$(3\text{-}3) \qquad Q_1 = Q_1(P_1, r, T)$$

The value of the default-free bond, Q_3, depends only on the rate of interest and time until maturity.

$$(3\text{-}4) \qquad Q_3 = Q_3(r, T)$$

The remaining asset, in the form of equity, is also assumed to be generated by an Ito process:

$$(3\text{-}5) \qquad \frac{dQ_2}{Q_2} = R_2 dt + \sigma_2 dz_2$$

Ito processes, although continuous, are not differentiable, and, thus, a tool is needed to manipulate functions that involve Ito processes. A thorough description of Ito processes is given in Ito and McKean (1964), but this discussion will focus only on Ito's lemma.

LEMMA Let $F + F(X_1, \ldots, X_n, t)$ be a function at least twice differentiable where the X_i's are generated by Ito processes, then its differential is given by:

$$(3\text{-}6) \qquad dF = \sum_{i=1}^{n} \frac{\partial F}{\partial X_i} dX_i + \frac{\partial F}{\partial t} dt + \frac{1}{2} \sum_{i=1}^{n} \sum_{i=1}^{n} \frac{\partial^2 F}{\partial X_i dX_j} dX_i dX_j$$

where the product $dX_i dX_j$ is defined by the rule

$$(3\text{-}7) \qquad dz_i dz_j = \rho_{ij} dt \qquad i, j = 1, \ldots, n$$

and

$$(3\text{-}8) \qquad dz_i dt = 0 \qquad i = 1, \ldots, n$$

and ρ_{ij} is the correlation coefficient between the Gauss-Weiner processes dz_i and dz_j.

Now, equipped with Ito's lemma, the percentage change in the commodity bond's price can be determined, as well as that of the default-free bond.

$$(3\text{-}9) \qquad dQ_1 = \frac{\partial Q_1}{\partial P_1} dP_1 + \frac{\partial Q_1}{\partial r} dr + \frac{\partial Q_1}{\partial T} + \frac{1}{2} \frac{\partial^2 Q_1}{\partial P_1^2} dP_1^2$$

$$+ \frac{1}{2} \frac{\partial^2 Q_1}{\partial r^2} dr^2 + \frac{\partial^2 Q_1}{\partial P_1 dr} dP_1 dr$$

However, T is defined as time until maturity, so that $dT = -dt$.

Furthermore, as an application of the multiplication rule given in Ito's lemma, the following products are obtained:

$$(3\text{-}10) \qquad dP_1^2 = P_1^2[\alpha_1 dt + s_1 dz_1]^2 = P_1^2 s_1^2 dt$$

$$(3\text{-}11) \qquad dr^2 = [\alpha_r dt + \sigma_r dz_r]^2 = \sigma_r^2 dt$$

$$(3\text{-}12) \qquad dP_1 dr = P_1[\sigma_1 dt + s_1 dz_1][\alpha_r dt + \sigma_r dz_r] = P_1 s_1 \sigma_r \rho_{1r} \, dt$$

With these new expressions, equation 3-9 becomes:

$$(3\text{-}13) \qquad \frac{\partial Q_1}{Q_1} = \left[\alpha_1 \frac{P_1}{Q_1} \frac{\partial Q_1}{\partial P_1} + \frac{\alpha_r}{Q_1} \frac{\partial Q_1}{\partial r} + \frac{1}{2} \frac{P_1^2 S_1^2}{Q_1} \frac{\partial^2 Q_1}{\partial P_1^2} + \frac{1}{2} \frac{\sigma_r^2}{Q_1} \frac{\partial^2 Q_1}{\partial r^2} \right.$$

$$\left. + \frac{P_1 S_1 \sigma_r}{Q_1} \rho_{1r} \frac{\partial^2 Q_1}{\partial P_1 \partial r} - \frac{1}{Q_1} \frac{\partial Q_1}{\partial T} \right] dt$$

$$+ \left[S_1 \frac{P_1}{Q_1} \frac{\partial Q_1}{\partial P_1} dz_1 + \frac{\partial r}{Q_1} \frac{\partial Q_1}{\partial r} dz_r \right]$$

Similar derivations for the default-free bond, yield:

$$(3\text{-}14) \qquad dQ_3 = \frac{\partial Q_3}{\partial r} dr + \frac{\partial Q_3}{\partial T} dT + \frac{1}{2} \frac{\partial^2 Q_3}{\partial r^2} dr^2$$

and

$$(3\text{-}15) \quad \frac{dQ_3}{Q_3} + \left[\frac{\alpha_r}{Q_3} \frac{\partial Q_3}{\partial r} + \frac{1}{2} \frac{\sigma_r^2}{Q_3} \frac{\partial^2 Q_3}{\partial r^2} - \frac{1}{Q_3} \frac{\partial Q_3}{\partial T} \right] dt + \frac{\sigma_r}{Q_3} \frac{\partial Q_3}{\partial r} dz_r$$

Furthermore, it is assumed that interest rates are nonstochastic so that $\sigma_r = 0$. The commodity bond's price elasticity is defined as

$$e_1 = \frac{P_1}{Q_1} \frac{\partial Q_1}{\partial P_1}.$$

As a result of these new specifications, asset returns are now fully expressed by:

$$(3\text{-}16) \quad \frac{dQ_1}{Q_1} = \left[\alpha_1 e_1 + \frac{\alpha_r}{Q_1} \frac{\partial Q_1}{\partial r} + \frac{1}{2} \frac{P_1^2 S_1^2}{Q_1} \frac{\partial^2 Q_1}{\partial P_1^2} - \frac{1}{Q_1} \frac{\partial Q_1}{\partial T} \right] dt + e_1 S_1 dz_1$$

$$(3\text{-}17) \quad \frac{dQ_1}{Q_1} = R_1 dt + \sigma_1 dz_1$$

$$(3\text{-}18) \quad \frac{dQ_2}{Q_2} = R_2 dt + \sigma_2 dz_2$$

$$(3\text{-}19) \quad \frac{dQ_3}{Q_3} = \left[\frac{\alpha_r}{Q_3} \frac{\partial Q_3}{\partial r} - \frac{1}{Q_3} \frac{\partial Q_3}{\partial T} \right] dt = R_3 dt = R_f dt$$

Budget Equation

To derive the individual's budget equation, the framework followed is one in which all the wealth is held in the assets, income is generated by capital gains, and the individual must reduce asset holdings to consume. A discrete model with time periods of length h is first developed before the continuous model is derived by taking h to 0.

Let $W(t)$ and $Q_i(t)$ be wealth and asset prices at the beginning of period t. $N_i(t)$ represents the number of shares of asset i held at date t. Thus,

$$(3\text{-}20) \quad W(t) = \sum_{i=1}^{3} N_i(t) Q_i(t)$$

To consume between dates t and $t + h$, the individual must reduce asset holdings at date t. All of that consumption is in the form of the commodity, according to this model, and $C(t)$ is the rate of consumption per unit time.

Consumption is thus given by:

$$(3\text{-}21) \quad \sum_{i=1}^{3} [N_i(t) - N_i(t + h)] Q_i(t) = P_1(t).C(t).h$$

Thus,

$$(3\text{-}22) \quad W(t + h) - W(t) = \sum_{i=1}^{3} N_i(t + h)Q_i(t + h) - \sum_{i=1}^{3} N_i(t)Q_i(t)$$

$$= \sum_{i=1}^{3} N_i(t + h)[Q_i(t + h) - Q_i(t)] - P_1(t).C(t).h$$

and

$$(3\text{-}23) \quad \frac{W(t + h) - W(t)}{h} = \sum_{i=1}^{3} N_i(t + h)\left[\frac{Q_i(t + h) - Q_i(t)}{h}\right]$$

$$- P_1(t).C(t)$$

As h goes to 0, the continuous version of this equation is as follows:

$$(3\text{-}24) \quad dW(t) = \sum_{i=1}^{3} N_i(t)dQ_i(t) - P_1(t).C(t).dt$$

Now introduced is ω_i, the proportion of the portfolio held in asset i.

$$(3\text{-}25) \quad \omega_i(t) = \frac{N_i(t)Q_i(t)}{W(t)}$$

Equation 3-24 becomes:

$$(3\text{-}26) \quad dW = \sum_{i=1}^{3} \omega_i W \frac{dQ_i}{Q_i} - P_1.C.dt$$

Using equation 3-18 and $\omega_3 = 1 - \sum_{i=1}^{2} \omega_i$, the budget equation becomes:

$$(3\text{-}27) \quad dW = \sum_{i=1}^{2} \omega_i W(R_i - R_f)dt + (WR_f - P_1C)dt + \sum_{i=1}^{2} \omega_1 W \sigma_i dz_i$$

Maximization Problem

Each individual is faced with the problem of choosing a portfolio and consumption pattern that will maximize the expected value of a time-additive von Neumann-Morgenstern utility function and bequest function.

The problem is formulated as:

$$(3\text{-}28) \quad \underset{(c, w_i)}{\text{Max } E_0}\left[\int_0^T U[C(t), t]dt + B[W(T), T]\right]$$

subject to equation 3-27 and $W(0) = W_0$.

The utility function U is assumed to be strictly concave in C, and the bequest function is strictly concave in W. The general technique used to solve these types of problems is that of dynamic programming, which is well described in Dreyfus (1965).

Now function J is introduced and defined by:

$$(3\text{-}29) \quad J(W, P_1, t) = \underset{(c, w_i)}{\text{Max}} E_t\left[\int_t^T U[C(T), T]\,dt + B[W(T), T]\right]$$

and

$$(3\text{-}30) \qquad \phi(w, c; W, P_1, t) = U[c(t), t] + L[J]$$

where L is the Dynkin operator over the variables W and P_1 for a given set of controls ω and C defined by:

$$(3\text{-}31) \quad L[J] = \frac{\partial J}{\partial t} = \left[\sum_{i=1}^{3} \omega_i R_i W - P_1 C\right]\frac{\partial J}{\partial W} + R_1 P_1 \frac{\partial J}{\partial P_1} + \frac{1}{2} S_{11} \frac{\partial^2 J}{\partial f P_1^2}$$

$$+ \frac{1}{2} \sum_{i=1}^{3}\sum_{j=1}^{3} \sigma_{ij}\omega_i\omega_j W^2 \frac{\partial^2 J}{\partial W^2} + \sum_{j=1}^{3} P_1 W \omega_j V_{1j} \frac{\partial^2 J}{\partial P_1 \partial W}$$

$\Omega = (\sigma_{ij})_{i,j}$ is the covariance matrix of asset returns and $V = (V_{1j})_j$ is the covariance vector of asset returns with the commodity price. Merton (1969) has shown that under the stated conditions here, optimal sets of controls exist and are found by differentiating the Lagrangian

$$(3\text{-}32) \qquad L = \phi + \lambda\left[1 - \sum_{i=1}^{3} \omega_i\right]$$

The first order conditions result in:

$$(3\text{-}33) \qquad 0 = U_c - P_1 J_W$$

$$(3\text{-}34) \quad 0 = -\lambda + R_1 W J_W + W^2 J_{WW}\left(\sum_{i=1}^{3} \sigma_{1i}\omega_i\right) + W P_1 V_{11} J^{1W}$$

$$(3\text{-}35) \quad 0 = -\lambda + R_2 W J_W + W^2 J_{WW}\left(\sum_{i=1}^{3} \sigma_{2i}\omega_i\right) + W P_1 V_{12} J_{1W}$$

$$(3\text{-}36) \quad 0 = -\lambda + R_3 W J_W + W^2 J_{WW}\left(\sum_{i=1}^{3} \sigma_{3i}\omega_i\right) + W P_1 V_{13} J_{1W}$$

$$(3\text{-}37) \qquad 0 = 1 - \sum_{i=1}^{3} \omega_i$$

where we note $F_x = \dfrac{\partial F}{\partial X}$.

The terms of the covariance matrices defined by $\sigma_{ij} = \rho_{ij}\sigma_i\sigma_j$ and the condition $\sigma_3 = 0$, however, imply that $\sigma_{3i} = 0$ for all i.

For a similar reason, $V_{ij} = \rho_{ij}S_i\sigma_j$ implies $V_{13} = 0$. The first-order conditions thus become:

$$(3\text{-}38) \qquad\qquad U_c = P_1 J_W$$

$$(3\text{-}39) \qquad 0 = (R_1 - R_f)J_W + WJ_{WW}\left(\sum_{i=1}^{2}\sigma_{1i}\omega_i\right) + P_1 J_{1W}V_{11}$$

$$(3\text{-}40) \qquad 0 = (R_2 - R_f)J_W + WJ_{WW}\sum_{i=1}^{2}\sigma_{2i}\omega_i + P_1 J_{1W}V_{12}$$

$$(3\text{-}41) \qquad\qquad \lambda = R_f W J_W$$

$$(3\text{-}42) \qquad\qquad 1 = \sum_{i=1}^{3}\omega_i$$

Demand Functions

The analysis just described the portfolio choice problem faced by an individual and enables the optimal asset portfolio to be derived.

Equation 3-38 states that, at the optimum, the marginal utility of consumption must equate the marginal utility of wealth. In matrix form, equations 3-39 and 3-40 can be rewritten:

$$(3\text{-}43) \quad \begin{vmatrix} \sigma_{11} & \sigma_{12} \\ \sigma_{12} & \sigma_{22} \end{vmatrix} \begin{vmatrix} \omega_1 W \\ \omega_2 W \end{vmatrix} = \frac{-J_W}{J_{WW}} \begin{vmatrix} R_1 - R_f \\ R_2 - R_f \end{vmatrix} - \frac{P_1 J_{1W}}{J_{WW}}\begin{vmatrix} V_{11} \\ V_{12} \end{vmatrix}$$

The various terms of the variance-covariance matrix are defined by:

$$(3\text{-}44) \qquad\qquad \sigma_{ij} = \rho_{ij}\sigma_i\sigma_j$$

ρ denotes the correlation coefficient between the commodity and the equity asset, so that

$$(3\text{-}45) \qquad\qquad \sigma_{12} = \rho\sigma_1\sigma_2$$

$$(3\text{-}46) \qquad\qquad \sigma_{11} = \sigma_1^2$$

$$(3\text{-}47) \qquad\qquad \sigma_{22} = \sigma_2^2$$

Furthermore, it is assumed that $\rho^2 \neq 1$, so that the variance-covariance matrix is nonsingular. The demand functions can now be derived for the various assets by matrix inversion in equation 3-43.

$$(3\text{-}48) \quad \begin{vmatrix} \omega_1 W \\ \omega_2 W \end{vmatrix} = \frac{-J_W}{J_{WW}\sigma_1^2\sigma_2^2(1-\rho^2)} \begin{vmatrix} \sigma_2^2 & -\rho\sigma_1\sigma_2 \\ -\rho\sigma_1\sigma_2 & \sigma_1^2 \end{vmatrix}\begin{vmatrix} R_1 - R_f \\ R_2 - R_f \end{vmatrix}$$

$$- \frac{P_1 J_{1W}}{J_{WW}\sigma_1^2\sigma_2^2(1-\rho^2)} \begin{vmatrix} \sigma_2^2 & -\rho\sigma_1\sigma_2 \\ -\rho\sigma_1\sigma_2 & \sigma_1^2 \end{vmatrix}\begin{vmatrix} \dfrac{s_1}{\sigma_1} & \sigma_1^2 \\ \dfrac{s_1}{\sigma_1} & \rho\sigma_1\sigma_2 \end{vmatrix}$$

and

(3-49) $$\omega_3 W = W - \omega_1 W - \omega_2 W$$

After simplifications, these equations are written:

(3-50) $$\omega_1 W = \frac{-J_W}{J_{WW}(1 - \rho^2)} \left[\frac{(R_1 - R_f)}{\sigma_1^2} - \rho \frac{(R_2 - R_f)}{\sigma_1 \sigma_2} \right] - \frac{P_1 J_{1W}}{J_{WW}} \frac{s_1}{\sigma_1}$$

(3-51) $$\omega_2 W = \frac{-J_W}{J_{WW}(1 - \rho^2)} \left[\frac{(R_2 - R_f)}{\sigma_2^2} - \rho \frac{(R_1 - R_f)}{\sigma_1 \sigma_2} \right]$$

(3-52) $$\omega_3 W = W - \omega_1 W - \omega_2 W$$

To express the last term of equation 3-50 as a function of the other variables, Fischer (1975) points out that the consumption decision by the individual is guided by commodity price changes relative to wealth, so that consumption is a function of real wealth.

(3-53) $$C = C(W/P_1, t)$$

By differentiating this equation to W and to P_1, one obtains:

(3-54) $$\frac{\partial C}{\partial W} = C_1 \frac{\partial(W/P_1)}{\partial W} = C_1 \frac{1}{P_1}$$

(3-55) $$\frac{\partial C}{\partial P_1} = C_1 \frac{\partial(W/P_1)}{\partial P_1} = -C_1 \frac{W}{P_1^2}$$

and thus the following relationship holds:

(3-56) $$\frac{\partial C}{\partial W} = \frac{-P_1}{W} \frac{\partial C}{\partial P_1}$$

Furthermore, when equation 3-38 is differentiated relative to W and to P_1, it yields:

(3-57) $$U_{CC} \frac{\partial C}{\partial P_1} = J_W + P_1 J_{1W}$$

(3-58)
$$U_{CC} \frac{\partial C}{\partial W} = P_1 J_{WW} = -U_{CC} \frac{P_1}{W} \frac{\partial C}{\partial P_1} = \frac{-P_1}{W} (J_W + P_1 J_{1W})$$

As a result,

(3-59) $$\frac{-P_1 J_{1W}}{J_{WW}} = W + \frac{J_W}{J_{WW}}$$

The individual's absolute risk tolerance T is defined as $T \equiv -U_c / U_{cc}$. Note that $T > 0$ because more is better ($U_C > 0$), and the utility function is assumed to be concave in C or the first units of consumption are worth more to the individual than the subsequent units.

Thus, $MT = -J_W/J_{WW}$ is defined as the individual's "modified" risk tolerance.

$$(3\text{-}60) \qquad \frac{-J_W}{J_{WW}} = \frac{-U_C}{U_{CC}\dfrac{\partial C}{\partial W}} = \frac{T}{\dfrac{\partial C}{\partial W}} = \frac{T}{C_W}$$

High values of this variable are obtained for high values of T and/or low values of the marginal propensity to consume. C_W can be expected to be a decreasing function of W. There could conceivably exist individuals for whom $C_W = 0$. These individuals have so much wealth that any increase in that wealth would not induce them to consume more. At the other extreme, very poor individuals would consume all of their additional gains, and, for them, $C_W = 1$, for at least W lower than a certain subsistence level.

With these simplifications, the demand equations for each individual k can be written:

$$(3\text{-}61) \quad \omega_1^k W^k = MT^k \left[\frac{(R_1 - R_f)}{(1 - \rho^2)\sigma_1^2} - \rho \frac{(R_2 - R_f)}{(1 - \rho^2)\sigma_1\sigma_2} \right] + \frac{1}{e_1}(W^K - MT^k)$$

$$(3\text{-}62) \qquad \omega_2^k W^k = MT^k \left[\frac{(R_2 - R_f)}{(1 - \rho^2)\sigma_2^2} - \rho \frac{(R_1 - R_f)}{(1 - \rho^2)\sigma_1\sigma_2} \right]$$

$$(3\text{-}63) \qquad \omega_3^k W^k = W^k - \omega_1^k W^k - \omega_2^k W^k$$

A look at the demand equations reveals that the demand for the equity asset is only comprised of a speculative component and is equal to the demand for a risky asset by a single period mean-variance maximizing investor. The demand for the commodity bond, however, is also comprised of a similar speculative component and a hedging component. A and B denote the bracket terms in equation 3-61 and 3-62, and these equations become:

$$(3\text{-}64) \qquad \omega_1^k W^k = MT^k . A + (W^k - MT^k)/e_1$$

$$(3\text{-}65) \qquad \omega_2^k W^k = MT^k . B$$

We define $MT^M = \sum_k MT^k$ as the market's modified risk tolerance.

By aggregating equations 3-64 and 3-65, one obtains:

$$(3\text{-}66) \qquad \omega_1^M . M = MT^M . A + (M - MT^M)/e_1$$

$$(3\text{-}67) \qquad \omega_2^M . M = MT^M . B$$

Substituting the values of A and B obtained from these equations back into equations 3-64 and 3-65, one is able to derive another expression for the demand functions:

(3-68) $$\omega_1^k W^k = \omega_1^M . M \frac{MT^k}{MT^M} + \frac{W^k}{e_1} \left[1 - \frac{MT^k/W^k}{MT^M/M} \right]$$

(3-69) $$\omega_2^k W^k = \omega_2^M . M \frac{MT^k}{MT^M}$$

The Determinants of the Demand for Commodity Bonds

Now consider the case in which the equity asset is the market portfolio before the introduction of commodity bonds. Modern portfolio theory indicates that investors would hold the market portfolio, levered up or down according to their aversion to risk. Two approaches can be taken here. One can analyze the change in the individual's portfolio mix after the introduction of a positive amount of commodity bonds or one can analyze and determine who would want to issue or hold such bonds, if they did not exist.

The latter approach will be taken here in justifying the introduction of such bonds. In this case, $\omega_1^M = 0$, and equation 3-68 becomes:

(3-70) $$\omega_1^k W^k = \frac{W^k}{e_1} \left[1 - \frac{MT^k/W^k}{MT^M/M} \right]$$

Thus, if $MT^k/W^k < MT^M/M$, then $\omega_1^k W^k > 0$. This is the result that is intuitively expected: When individual k has a lower relative modified risk tolerance than the market or a higher relative modified risk aversion, the individual would have a positive demand for commodity bonds.

A comparison of equations 3-70 and 3-64, however, reveals that, even in this case, the demand for commodity bonds is not limited to the hedging component. Samuelson (1985) points out that sellers of such bonds will be those least averse to price risk as they are bribed to take on some of the irreducible variability by an appropriate market-clearing premium. For such individuals, their attitude toward commodity bonds will be guided by their speculative demand. Samuelson also notes that if the supply of commodity bonds were to come only from individuals willing to take a little more risk for a premium, the market for commodity bonds would not be viable. This market must also be driven by a commercial function with the involvement of major players, big corporations, or governments, which are seeking to hedge the variations in their production costs or revenues.

Now take a closer look at the determinants of the demand for commodity bonds. From equation 3-61, it can be seen that the determinants depend on the required rates of return for three assets: the correlation between the commodity and the market, their respective volatilities, and the individual's modified risk tolerance.

From this point on, D_i^k will denote individual k's demand for asset i:

(3-71) $$D_i^k = \omega_i^k W^k$$

In taking the partial derivative of equation 3-61 with respect to R_1, one obtains:

(3-72) $$\frac{\partial D_1^k}{\partial R_1} = \frac{MT^k}{(1 - \rho^2)\sigma_1^2} > 0$$

This is a general property of most demand functions as they are decreasing with respect to price. Equation 3-72 indicates that if R_1 increases or the price of the commodity bond goes down, the demand for it will go up.

Before taking the partial of equation 3-61 with respect to R_2, note that whenever $\rho > 0$, the market serves as a hedge against inflation in the sense that the value of this asset goes up at the same time that investors need it the most: when commodity prices go up.

(3-73) $$\frac{\partial D_1^k}{\partial R_2} = \frac{-\rho MT^k}{(1 - \rho^2)\sigma_1\sigma_2}$$

Therefore, if $\rho > 0$, $\dfrac{\partial D_1^k}{\partial R_2}$ is implied. In other words, whenever R_2 decreases or Q_2 goes up, the demand for commodity bonds will also go up. Thus, when $\rho > 0$, commodity bonds and the market act as substitutes.

(3-74) $$\frac{\partial D_1^k}{\partial R_f} = \frac{MT^k}{(1 - \rho^2)\sigma_1^2\sigma_2}(\rho\sigma_1 - \sigma_2)$$

The commodity bond's market beta is introduced and defined as:

(3-75) $$\beta_1 = \frac{\text{cov}(\tilde{\varepsilon}_1, \tilde{\varepsilon}_2)}{\text{var}(\tilde{\varepsilon}_2)} = \frac{\rho\sigma_1}{\sigma_2}$$

and notice that when $\beta_1 > 1$, it implies $\rho\sigma_1 - \sigma_2 > 0$.

Equation 3-74 indicates that when default-free bond prices go down so that R_f goes up, there will be a greater demand for commodity bonds when their market beta is greater than 1. Remembering that $\sigma_1 = e_1s_1$, the commodity bonds' market beta is e_1 times the commodity's market beta.

(3-76) $$\frac{\partial D_1^k}{\partial \sigma_1} = \frac{MT^k}{(1 - \rho^2)\sigma_1^2}\left[\rho\frac{(R_2 - R_f)}{\sigma_2} - 2\frac{(R_1 - R_f)}{\sigma_1}\right]$$

By using a continuous-time framework, Breeden (1979) derived an intertemporal pricing relationship that must hold at each instant in time:

$$(3\text{-}77) \qquad\qquad R_1 - R_f = \frac{\beta_{1c}}{\beta_{2c}}(R_2 - R_f)$$

where β_{ic} is the consumption-beta for asset i, defined by:

$$(3\text{-}78) \qquad\qquad \beta_{ic} = \frac{\text{cov}\,(\tilde{\varepsilon}_i,\, d\ln \tilde{C})}{\text{var}\,(d\ln C)}$$

With the use of these relationships, equation 3-76 becomes:

$$(3\text{-}79) \qquad \frac{\partial D_1^k}{\partial \sigma_1} = \frac{MT^k.\,(R_2 - R_f)}{(1 - \rho^2)\sigma_1^2}\left[\frac{\rho}{\sigma_2} - \frac{2}{\sigma_1}\frac{\beta_{1c}}{\beta_{2c}}\right]$$

This still assumes $\rho > 0$. A similar analysis can be made for $\rho < 0$. In general, $\beta_{2c} > 0$ as individuals increase their rate of consumption when the market is going up. The sign of β_{1c} is ambiguous, however. If commodity prices and consumption are correlated negatively, which is what would happen if higher commodity prices induced individuals to reduce their rate of consumption, equation 3-79 indicates a greater demand for commodity bonds when commodity prices become more volatile. Such would be the case as long as

$$(3\text{-}80) \qquad\qquad \beta_{1c} < \rho\beta_{2c}\sigma_1/2\sigma_2$$

Furthermore,

$$(3\text{-}81) \qquad\qquad \frac{\partial D_1^k}{\partial \sigma_2} = \frac{\rho MT^k(R_2 - R_f)}{(1 - \rho^2)\sigma_1\sigma_2^2}$$

When ρ is positive, it has been shown that the market and commodity bonds act as substitutes. As the market becomes more volatile, it is a less accurate hedge against price changes. This increases the demand for commodity bonds.

$$(3\text{-}82) \qquad \frac{\partial D_1^k}{\partial \rho} = \frac{MT^k}{\sigma_1(1 - \rho^2)^2}\left[2\rho\frac{(R_1 - R_f)}{\sigma_1} - (1 + \rho^2)\frac{(R_2 - R_f)}{\sigma_2}\right]$$

In using Breeden's intertemporal pricing relationship, equation 3-82 becomes:

$$(3\text{-}83) \qquad \frac{\partial D_1^k}{\partial \rho} = \frac{MT^k(R_2 - R_f)}{\sigma_1(1 - \rho^2)^2}\left[\frac{2\rho}{\sigma_1}\frac{\beta_{1C}}{\beta_{2c}} - \frac{(1 - \rho^2)}{\sigma_2}\right]$$

With the above-stated assumptions of $\rho > 0$ and $\beta_{1C} < \rho\,\beta_{2C}\,\sigma_1/2\sigma_2$, one notes that $\partial D_1^k/\partial \rho > 0$. An intuitive explanation lies in the fact that when the commodity's correlation with the market decreases, the market becomes a less desirable hedging tool. Furthermore, it can easily be shown that when ρ decreases, the variance of the total portfolio decreases due to the inclusion of commodity bonds. As a result, the latter become more attractive.

The previous analysis derived in the case of a single-good economy is also valid when relative commodity prices are fixed and individuals consume the same consumption bundle. In that case, the commodity bond described would be a CPI-bond. These assumptions are very restrictive, however, because commodity prices are known to fluctuate somewhat independently, and individuals have differing tastes. The next section thus extends the analysis to the case of a multigood economy with stochastic consumption opportunities.

The Multigood Case

The model presented in this section is a multigood extension of the previous analysis. There have been very few attempts to extend Merton's intertemporal asset pricing model and incorporate the case of many consumption goods. Long (1974) took such an approach, but only in the case of a discrete-time economy. A satisfactory extension was made by Breeden (1979, 1984) in the derivation of a consumption asset pricing model and in the examination of the allocational roles of futures markets in a multigood and multiperiod economy and by Cox, Ingersoll, and Ross (1985).

The Model

All the assumptions made in the single-good case are repeated in this section for a description of the economy. One can now examine the case in which there are m consumption goods, among which l are commodity goods with $l \leq m$. The price dynamics for these goods are assumed to be generated by Ito processes.

$$(3\text{-}84) \qquad \frac{dP_j}{P_j} = a_j dt + s_j dx_j \quad j = 1, \ldots, m$$

where a_j and s_j are constant.

There are n assets with returns that are also assumed to be generated by Ito processes. The first l assets are commodity bonds with $l \leq m \leq n$.

$$(3\text{-}85) \qquad \frac{dQ_i}{Q_i} = R_i dt + \sigma_i dz_i \quad i = 1, \ldots, n$$

The default-free bond's return is given by

$$(3\text{-}86) \qquad \frac{dQ_{n+1}}{Q_{n+1}} = R_{n+1} dt = R_f dt$$

Along the same lines as the single-good case, each commodity bond is a function of its own commodity price, the interest rate, and the time until maturity.

$$(3\text{-}87) \qquad Q_i = Q_i(P_i, r, T_i) \quad i = 1, \dots, l$$

As an application of Ito's lemma, it is easy to see that $dx_j = dz_j$ for $j = 1, \dots, l$ and that each commodity bond is perfectly correlated with its own commodity price.

C_j^k denotes the rate of consumption of good j by individual k by C_j^k, and

$$e^k = \sum_{j=1}^{m} P_j C_j^k$$

is defined as the individual's rate of nominal expenditure. An analysis similar to that of the previous section shows that individual k's budget constraint is given by

$$(3\text{-}88) \quad dW^k = \sum_{i=1}^{n} \omega_i^k(R_i - R_f)W^k dt + (W^k R_f - e^k)dt + \sum_{i=1}^{n} \omega_i^k W^k \sigma_i dz_i$$

or in matrix form

$$(3\text{-}89) \qquad dW^k = \omega^k(R_a - R_f)W^k dt + (W^k R_f - e^k)dt + W^k \omega^k \sigma_a dz_a$$

where ω^k is the portfolio weights vector for individual k, R_a the assets return vector, σ_a the $n \times n$ diagonal matrix of assets standard deviation, and dz_a the Gauss-Weiner processes vector.

At each instant, individual k is assumed to maximize a time additive von Neumann-Morgenstern utility function given by,

$$(3\text{-}90) \qquad E_0\left[\int_0^{} T^k u^k(C^k, Y)dY + P^k[W^k(T^k), T^k]\right]$$

where C^k denotes the rate of consumption vector for individual k: $C^k = (C_j^k)_j$. Let $U^k(e^k, P', t) = \text{Max } u^k(C^k, t)$ describe individual k's indirect utility function for consumption expenditures and P' the transpose of the consumption-good price vector. The dynamic programming methodology described in the previous section, yields the following first-order conditions:

$$(3\text{-}91) \qquad U_e^k(e^k, P', t) = J_W^k(W^k, S', t)$$

$$(3\text{-}92) \qquad \omega^k W^k = \frac{-J_W^k}{J_{WW}^k} V_{aa}^{-1}(R_a - R_f) - V_{aa}^{-1}V_{as}\frac{J_{SW}^k}{J_{WW}^k}$$

where S' is the transpose of the state variables vector (that is, variables that describe the investment, income, and consumption opportunities sets), V_{aa} is the $n \times n$ variance-covariance matrix of asset returns, and V_{as} the $n \times m$ covariance matrix of asset returns with the state variables.

The Demand Functions

From this point onward, the commodity prices are chosen to be the state variables. By differentiating equation 3-91 with respect to W, one obtains:

$$(3\text{-}93) \qquad U_{ee}^k(e^k, P', t) \cdot e_W^k = J_{WW}^k(W^k, S', t)$$

Equations 3-91 and 3-93 combined, yield:

$$(3\text{-}94) \qquad \frac{-J_W^k}{J_{WW}^k} = \frac{-U_e^k}{U_{ee}^k \cdot e_W^k} = MT^k$$

The last term in equation 3-92 denoted

$$H_S^k = \frac{-J_{SW}^k}{J_{WW}^k}$$

was shown by Merton (1973a) to represent individual k's hedging demands against adverse changes in the consumption-investment opportunity set. Equation 3-92 thus becomes:

$$(3\text{-}95) \qquad \omega^k W^k = MT^k V_{aa}^{-1}(R_a - R_f) + V_{aa}^{-1} V_{as} H_s^k$$

by aggregating across all individuals, one obtains:

$$(3\text{-}96) \qquad \omega^M W^M = MT^M V_{aa}^{-1}(R_a - R_f) + V_{aa}^{-1} V_{as} H_s^M$$

where

$$(3\text{-}97) \qquad H_S^M = \sum_k H_s^k.$$

Equations 3-95 and 3-96 together present a new expression for the asset demand functions:

$$(3\text{-}98) \qquad \omega^k W^k = \frac{MT^k \cdot M}{MT^M} \omega^M + V_{aa}^{-1} V_{as}\left(H_s^k - \frac{MT^k \cdot H_S^M}{MT^M} \right)$$

With an argument similar to that of the previous section, the net demand for any commodity bond across the market should be zero, thereby yielding $\omega_i^M = 0$ for $i = 1, \ldots, l$. Furthermore, Breeden (1979) has shown that $V_{aa}^{-1} V_{as}$ has, for columns, the portfolio of assets most highly correlated with the state variables; here, those state variables are the commodity prices. Hence, column j gives the portfolio that has the maximum correlation with state variable P_j. As an application of Ito's lemma, it is evident that this price is perfectly correlated with commodity bond Q_j. Thus $V_{aa}^{-1} V_{as} = \left(\begin{smallmatrix} \Gamma \\ 0 \end{smallmatrix} \right)$, where Γ is an $l \times l$ diagonal matrix that can be normalized to unity by proper scaling of state variables. With these new results, equation 3-98 can be rewritten:

$$(3\text{-}99) \qquad \omega_i^k W^k = H_i^k - \frac{MT^k H_i^M}{MT^M} \quad i = 1, \ldots, l$$

and

$$(3\text{-}100) \qquad \omega_i^k W_k = \frac{MT^k . M}{MT^M} \omega_i^M \quad i = l+1, \ldots, n$$

These equations are similar to equations 3-69 and 3-70 derived in the single-consumption-good case. To obtain the exact link between the two sets of equations, H_i^k must be expressed in terms of known parameters. To that effect, the additional assumption that individuals have time-additive isoelastic utility functions is introduced. Under this condition, Dieffenbach (1976) has shown that individual k's vector of percentage compensating variations in wealth for changes in the state variables is not a function of k's wealth level, or:

$$(3\text{-}101) \qquad \frac{J_i^k}{W^k J^k W} = -\lambda_i^k$$

where λ_i^k does not depend on W_k, but does, in general, depend on the P_js. By differentiating with respect to W^k, one obtains:

$$(3\text{-}102) \qquad J_{iw}^k W^k J_W^k - J_i^k [J_W^k + W^k J_{WW}^k] = 0$$

Replacing J_i^k with its expression from equation 3-101, the condition becomes:

$$(3\text{-}103) \qquad J_{iw}^k = -\lambda_i^k [J_W^k + W^k J_{WW}^k]$$

or

$$(3\text{-}104) \qquad H_i^k = \frac{-J_{iW}^k}{J_{WW}^k} = \lambda_i^k (W^k - MT^k)$$

By aggregating across individuals, one obtains:

$$(3\text{-}105) \qquad H_i^M = \lambda_i^M . M - \lambda_{i,T}^M MT^M$$

where $\lambda_i^M = \frac{1}{M} \sum_k \lambda_i^k W^k$ and $\lambda_{i,T}^M = \frac{1}{MT^M} \sum_k \lambda_i^k MT^k$. Therefore, the demand for commodity bonds is given by

$$(3\text{-}106) \quad \omega_i^k W^k = \lambda_i^k W^k - \lambda_i^k MT^k - \frac{MT^k . M}{MT^M} \lambda_i^M + MT^k \lambda_{i,T}^M$$

By rearranging these terms, a more useful expression for the demand for commodity bonds can be derived.

$$(3\text{-}107) \quad \omega_i^k W^k = \lambda_i^k W^k \left[1 - \frac{MT^k/W^k}{MT^M/M} + MT^k \left(\frac{M}{MT^M} - 1 \right) (\lambda_i^k - \lambda_I^M) \right.$$

$$\left. + MT^k (\lambda_{i,T}^M - \lambda_i^M) \right]$$

The demand for commodity bonds is thus comprised of three terms, the first of which is similar to the expression obtained in equation 3-70. The reason for this is that if all individuals consumed the same bundle in the same quantities, λ_i^k would be equal across individuals, and $\lambda_i^k = \lambda_{i,}$ implies both $\lambda_i^M = \lambda_i$ and $\lambda_{i,T}^M = \lambda_i$ so the last two terms of equation 3-107 cancel out. Futhermore, when all individuals consume the same bundle, it can be considered as one consumption good, and the same results are found as in the previous section. This first term examined has a positive contribution to the demand for commodity bonds whenever individual k has a lower relative risk tolerance than the market or a higher relative risk aversion. The second term reveals that when the market is relatively more risk averse than unity, individual k would have an additional demand for commodity bond i when the individual is more affected than the average individual by changes in that commodity's price. This would tend to be the case for commodities for which individual k has a very inelastic demand. The sign of the last term is the same for all individuals and does not play a major role in the analysis of the demand for commodity bonds.

4

A Review of Methods for Pricing Commodity-Linked Securities

Theophilos Priovolos

The model for pricing commodity-linked securities uses the option pricing framework as pioneered by Black and Scholes (1973), extended by Merton (1973b) and Cox and Ross (1976), and further refined by Schwartz (1982). The model for pricing commodity-convertible bonds uses the option pricing framework of commodity-linked bonds[1] or the model of pricing convertible bonds as presented among others by Brennan and Schwartz (1980). As commodity-convertible bonds are equivalent to appropriately specified commodity bonds without warrants, the discussion here focuses only on the latter type of bonds. The key assumption of the model is that the underlying commodities, the commodity-linked bonds, and the equities of the firm issuing the bonds are continuously traded in frictionless markets.

The Schwartz model considers commodity price risk, default risk, and interest rate risk and takes the form of a second-order partial differential equation in four variables that governs the value of the commodity-linked bond at any point in time. Let P be the value of the reference commodity bundle, V the value of the firm issuing the bonds, and r the instantaneously riskless rate of interest and assume that they follow continuous paths described by the following stochastic differential equations:

$$(4\text{-}1) \qquad \frac{dP}{P} = \alpha_p \, dt + \sigma_p \, dz_p$$

$$(4\text{-}2) \qquad \frac{dV}{V} = \left(\alpha_v - \frac{D(V, t)}{V} \right) dt + \sigma_v \, dz_v$$

$$(4\text{-}3) \qquad dr = \alpha_r(r) \, dt + \sigma_r(r) \, dz_r$$

where D is the rate of total payouts of all the security holders of the firm (dividends, interest, etc.); σ_p, σ_r are constants; and dz_p, dz_v, and dz_r are Gauss-Weiner processes with

(4-4) $dz_p \cdot dz_v = \rho\, dt,\; dz_p \cdot dz_r = \rho_{pr} \cdot dt,\; dz_v \cdot dz_r = \rho_{vr} \cdot dt$

The total value of the commodity-linked bond can be expressed as

(4-5) $$B = B(P, V, r, T)$$

where T is the time until maturity. If a portfolio is formed by investing

X_1 in the underlying commodity, P
X_2 in the firm, V
X_3 in a riskless discount bond, G
X_4 in the commodity-linked bond,[2] B

then the instantaneous total return on this portfolio dY will be

(4-6) $$dY = X_1 \frac{dP}{P} + X_2 \frac{dV + D\,dt}{V} + X_3 \frac{dG}{G} + X_4 \frac{dB + C\,dt}{B}$$

G is assumed to depend only on r and T, that is, $G(r, T)$; c is the coupon payment of the commodity bond. By applying Ito's lemma, one obtains:

(4-7) $$\frac{dG}{G} = \alpha_G \, dt + \sigma_G \, dz_r$$

If we apply Ito's lemma in 4-5 and introduce the result in 4-6 with 4-1, 4-2, and 4-7 and choose X_1, X_2, X_3, X_4 so that the portfolio return becomes riskless, the following partial differential equation governing the value of the commodity-linked bond at every point in time is derived:

(4-8) $\frac{1}{2}\sigma_p^2 P^2 B_{pp} + \frac{1}{2}\sigma_v^2 V^2 B_{vv} + \frac{1}{2}\sigma_r^2 B_{rr} + \sigma_{pv} PV B_{pv} + \sigma_{pr} PB_{pr}$

   $+\; \sigma_{vr} VB_{vr} + rPB_p + (rV - D)B_v + (\alpha_r - \lambda\sigma_r)B_r - B_T - rB + C = 0$

The value of the bonds will be independent of the expected return on the commodity and on the firm; it will only depend on the current values of the reference commodity bundles and the firm (P, V). The promised payment on the bonds at maturity is equivalent to the face value of the bond (F), plus an option to buy the reference commodity bundle at a specified exercise price (E). The promised payment can be made only if the value of the firm at maturity is greater than that amount.

It is assumed that in case of default, the bondholder takes over the firm. The boundary condition at maturity can be expressed as

(4-9) $$B(P, V, r, 0) = \min\,[V, F + \max\,(0, P - E)]$$

Because the solution of 4-8 and 4-9 is very difficult, the following three simplified versions of the model can be obtained.

Case 1: Uncertain Commodity Price

Under the assumptions of no-default risk and constant interest rates, the solution of 4-8 subject to 4-9 gives

$$(4\text{-}10) \qquad B(P, T) = \frac{C}{r}(1 - e^{-rT}) + Fe^{-rT} + W(P, T)$$

where $W(P, T)$ is the Black-Scholes solution to the value of a call option with exercise price E.[3]

If C/F is the coupon rate that the issuer must offer to sell the bonds (face value at time of issue T), then 4-10 can be written as:

$$(4\text{-}11) \qquad \frac{C}{F} = r - \frac{r}{(1 - e^{-rT})} \cdot \frac{W(P, T)}{F}$$

The issuer has three parameters to influence the price of the bond at the time of the issue: the coupon rate (C/F), the exercise price (E), and the amount of the commodity to be included in the reference bundle.

Case 2: Default Risk

In case 2, there is a constant interest rate, only one commodity bond, and zero dividends paid. In this case, if S is the total value of equity of the firm; that is,

$$(4\text{-}12) \qquad\qquad V = B + S$$

then, the boundary condition can be rewritten as

$$(4\text{-}13) \qquad S(P, V, 0) = \begin{array}{ll} \max(0, V - F) & \text{for } P \le E \\ \max(0, V - P + E - F) & \text{for } P > E \end{array}$$

Solving 4-8 subject to 4-12 and 4-13, the value of commodity-linked bonds can be derived as

$$(4\text{-}14) \qquad B(P, V, T) = V(1 - M_{a1} - M_{b3}) + e^{-rT}F(M_{a2} + M_{b5})$$
$$+ PM_{b4} - e^{rT}E \cdot M_{b5}$$

where M_{a1} to M_{b5} are integrals of transformation of F, V, r, T, E, P, inter alia. This bond value includes the default risk in addition to commodity price risk.

Case 3: Interest Rate Risk

In case 3, there is no default risk and a stochastic interest rate. If $Q(T)$ replaces the default-free discount bond $G(r, T)$ and its growth rate is appropriately replaced in 4-6, then the derived new 4-8 function may be solved subject to the boundary condition

(4-15) $B(P, r, 0) = F + \max(0, P - E)$

If the commodity-linked bond is of the discount type, its value can be expressed as

(4-16) $B(P, Q, T) = F \cdot Q + W(P, Q, T)$

where the value of option $W(P, Q, T)$ can be obtained from Merton (1973b).

Several numerical examples by Schwartz (1982) using cases 1 to 3 show interesting properties of commodity bonds. In case 1, the higher the standard deviation of the commodity price (σ_p), the higher the value of the option (W) and the lower the required coupon rate (C/F). When the value of the reference bundle $(P|F)$ becomes zero, the bond becomes riskless, and C/F equates to r. When $P|F = 1$, that is, the value of the reference bundle equals the face value of the bond, the equilibrium coupon rate is negative.

In case 2, the boundary condition indicates that default at maturity depends not only on the value of the firm, but also on the value of the commodity bundle. A higher standard deviation on the return on the commodity (σ_p) has two opposing effects on bond values: First, it is well known that the value of an option increases with the standard deviation of its underlying security; second, the probability of default also increases with σ_p, and this tends to lower bond values. The first effect dominates the second for low commodity bundle prices, for high firm values, and for shorter maturity dates. Default risk thus has a significant impact on bond values, and most of this risk comes not from the firm being unable to pay the face value of the commodity bonds, as in the case for regular corporate bonds, but from the firm being unable to pay the value of the option for high commodity prices even under substantial increases in the value of the firm. A higher correlation between the return on the commodity and the return on the firm increases bond values. As the risk of default decreases, the value of the bond approaches the solution for the no-default, constant-interest-rate case.

The analysis involving case 3 shows that when pricing commodity bonds, it is quite safe to use the constant interest rate model as long as the relevant interest rate used is the one to the maturity of the bond.

It is noteworthy that some of the assumptions used to derive the Schwartz model are questionable. The model assumes, for example, that the underlying commodity is perfectly tradable. The model neglects taxes completely. Also, like most of the option pricing literature, the model assumes constant variances. More complex capital structures and bond characteristics—such as call features, sinking funds, and convertibility into the reference commodity bundle before maturity if convertible commodity bonds are considered—could be introduced at the cost of having to use complicated numerical procedures to solve the appropriate partial differential operations.[4]

The next section describes pricing commodity bonds with the use of binomial option pricing. This method has a number of advantages over the Schwartz approach.

Notes

1. A commodity-convertible bond can be shown to be equivalent to an appropriately specified commodity bond with "American"-type warrants.

2. The commodity-linked bond is a conventional bond with commodity (call) warrants attached to coupon or principal payments.

3. The Black-Scholes formula is

$$W(P, T) = PN(x) - Er^{-T}N(x - \sigma\sqrt{T}) \text{ where}$$

$$x = \frac{\log(P/Er^{-T})}{\sigma\sqrt{T}} + \frac{1}{2}\sigma\sqrt{T}.$$

4. Fall (1986) extends the Schwartz model by including the convenience yield of holding and storing the commodity. He argues that his version is more reliable. Brennan (1986) has, however, shown that convenience yields are very difficult to estimate. This could be the reason for the differences in the pricing of commodity bonds between Schwartz and Fall.

5

Pricing Commodity Bonds Using Binomial Option Pricing

Raghuram Rajan

Interest in commodity-linked securities has increased considerably recently. For the developing countries, these securities offer the possibility of hedging against commodity price risk, thereby enhancing their creditworthiness. Such instruments also link debt repayments to ability to pay (Priovolos, 1987a).

Conventional bonds pay a stated interest rate (coupon) and a fixed principal redeemable at maturity. A commodity bond makes repayments subject to the fluctuations in the price of the underlying commodity. Thus, both the coupon and the principal repayment may be a function of the commodity price. A variety of commodity-bond-type instruments can be devised, resulting in different kinds of risk sharing and return. Two of the more popular variants are the Commodity Convertible Bond (CCB) and the Commodity Linked Bond (CLB). With the CCB, the holder can choose on redemption day either the nominal face value or a prespecified amount of the commodity bundle. The CLB consists of a conventional bond with an attached option or warrant to buy a certain amount of the commodity at a predetermined exercise price. In some markets (not in the United States), the option can be detached and sold separately. In return for the convertibility/option feature, the issuer receives a lower interest rate.

Issues of commodity bonds can assist liability management by tailoring payments to ability to pay. In a CCB/CLB, the coupon provides a "floor" yield. When the price of the commodity increases, however, the yield to maturity for the bond increases and vice versa when the commodity price falls (limited by the floor level).

Formulas for pricing commodity-linked bonds have been developed by Schwartz (1982) and Carr (1987). Both use the standard continuous-time option pricing method to arrive at a differential equation. The extended form of the differential equation (incorporating convenience yields) is shown in appendix 5-1. Schwartz states that the solution to the general problem is difficult even by numerical methods and proceeds to make simplifying assumptions about the nature of the bond to obtain a solution. Even the simplified form of the bond has a mathematically complex, closed-form solution. The need for a simpler, more intuitive, and flexible formulation has been felt.

This chapter presents a method for pricing commodity-linked bonds in the presence of default risk and commodity price risk. The advantage of this method is that extensions are very simple. Further, the method is more intuitive than the continuous-time method, although it is equivalent in the limit. Most important, it is flexible and comprehensive. Finally, it can be used to model any bond instrument based on two or more stochastic processes.

Evnine (1983) first extended the Cox, Ross, and Rubinstein option pricing model to incorporate an option on two or more stocks. The model developed here is basically a simplification and reformulation of Evnine's model and an application of the model to commodity bonds.

In "The Model," a simple version of the bond is priced to make the process transparent. In "Parameter Determination," the parameters of the model are derived from real world values. In "Extensions," the model is extended to incorporate the various features that these bonds can include. In "Comparative Analysis of Binomial Model and Schwartz Model Results," some values obtained by the model are compared with those obtained by Schwartz. Further, some of the additional features are added and priced, and observations about some interesting phenomena are made. While appendix 5-1 describes the differential equation that has to be solved and Schwartz's solution to the simplified form, appendix 5-2 shows the logic behind the values of the chosen parameters.

The Model

Assumptions

(1) The commodity-linked bond consists of a zero coupon paying face value F at maturity, plus an option to buy a predefined quantity of the commodity with value at maturity date equal to P^* at an exercise price of E.[1] The option is European,[2] with the maturity date the same as the redemption date.

(5-1) $B^* = F + \max\,[0, P^* - E]$

where B^* is what the bond ought to pay at maturity.

(2) At maturity, however, the firm's value V^* (consisting of the total

value of its assets to its creditors) may be greater than or less than B^*. If the firm is unable to pay, the bondholders get the residual value of the firm.[3]

Therefore, the value of the bond is equal to:

(5-2) $\min [V^*, F + \max (0, P^* - E)]$

(3) There are no payouts from the firm to the shareholders or bondholders before the maturity date of the bond.

(4) The commodity bundle price and the firm value follow multiplicative binomial processes[4] over discrete periods.

(5) The interest rate is constant and positive.

(6) The firm's debt consists only of commodity bonds; that is, there is no senior debt.

(7) No taxes or transaction costs exist, and short sales are allowed. Further, assets are perfectly divisible.

(8) There is no convenience yield from the commodity. Assumptions (1), (3), (5), (6), and (8) can be relaxed.

Let the price of the commodity bundle and the value of the firm follow the continuous-time diffusion processes described below:

(5-3) $$\frac{dP}{P} = \mu_p \, dt + \sigma_p \, dz_p$$

(5-4) $$\frac{dV}{V} = \mu_v \, dt + \sigma_v \, dz_v$$

(5-5) $$dz_p \, dz_v = \sigma_{pv} \, dt$$

Where σ_p is the volatility of the commodity price, σ_v is the volatility of the firm value, and σ_{pv} is the covariance between the two. Also μ_p and μ_v are the drifts of the corresponding price movements.

In this model, the continuous-time diffusion processes will be approximated with binomial jumps.

If the commodity price and firm value moved independently, it would be easy to model the two as a two-step sequence of independent jumps. To introduce the covariance term, however, a third step is needed in which the price of the commodity bundle and the firm value move together (i.e., because there are two underlying stochastic processes and the processes are not independent, a three-step process will be assumed).

Assume three assets: the commodity bundle with price P, the firm with value V, and a risk-free bond of face value B. Let $\hat{r}$ be $1+$ the riskless rate of return per period. (Each jump is considered to occur in a period.)

STEP 1.   Price of commodity bundle P moves up by u_1 with probability q_1 or down by d_1 with probability $(1 - q_1)$. The value of the firm V accrues at the riskless rate $\hat{r}$. This is because there is no uncertainty about

Figure 5-1 *The Binomial Tree*

At the end of each three-step unit, the values of the two state variables P and V are as follows.

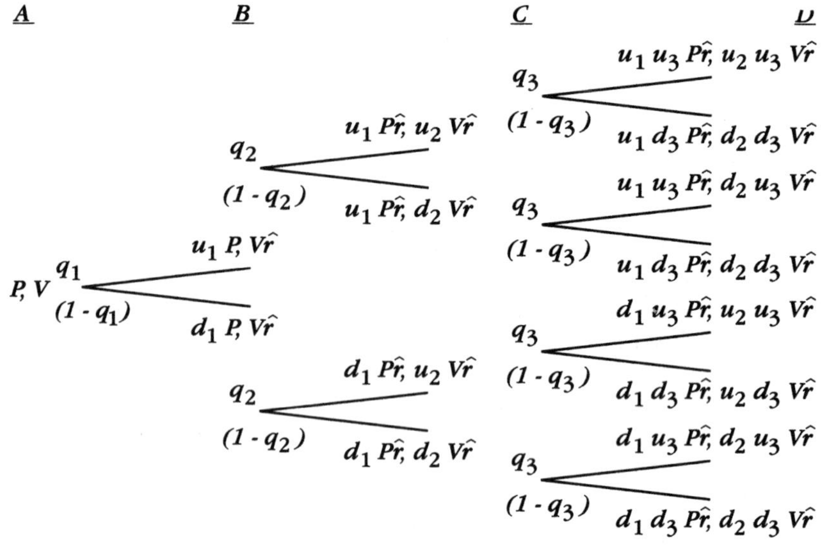

<u>A</u>   <u>B</u>   <u>C</u>   <u>D</u>

$$q_3 \quad u_1\, u_3\, P\hat{r},\ u_2\, u_3\, V\hat{r}$$
$$u_1\, P\hat{r},\ u_2\, V\hat{r} \quad (1-q_3) \quad u_1\, d_3\, P\hat{r},\ d_2\, d_3\, V\hat{r}$$
$$q_2$$
$$(1-q_2) \quad u_1\, P\hat{r},\ d_2\, V\hat{r} \quad q_3 \quad u_1\, u_3\, P\hat{r},\ d_2\, u_3\, V\hat{r}$$
$$u_1\, P,\ V\hat{r} \quad (1-q_3) \quad u_1\, d_3\, P\hat{r},\ d_2\, d_3\, V\hat{r}$$
$$q_1$$
$$P, V$$
$$(1-q_1) \quad d_1\, P,\ V\hat{r} \quad d_1\, u_3\, P\hat{r},\ u_2\, u_3\, V\hat{r}$$
$$q_3$$
$$d_1\, P\hat{r},\ u_2\, V\hat{r} \quad (1-q_3) \quad d_1\, d_3\, P\hat{r},\ u_2\, d_3\, V\hat{r}$$
$$q_2$$
$$(1-q_2) \quad d_1\, P\hat{r},\ d_2\, V\hat{r} \quad d_1\, u_3\, P\hat{r},\ d_2\, u_3\, V\hat{r}$$
$$q_3$$
$$(1-q_3) \quad d_1\, d_3\, P\hat{r},\ d_2\, d_3\, V\hat{r}$$

The bond values at the end of the third step are as shown below.

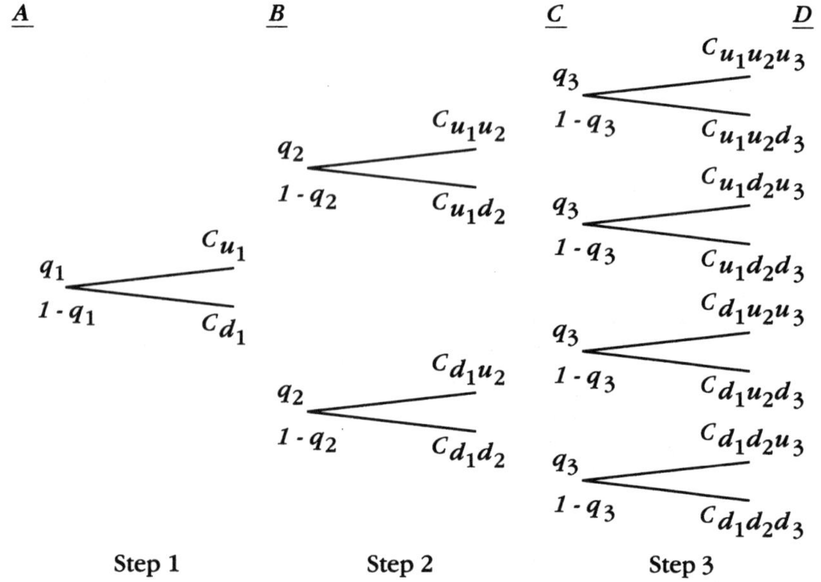

<u>A</u>   <u>B</u>   <u>C</u>   D

$$q_3 \quad C_{u_1 u_2 u_3}$$
$$C_{u_1 u_2} \quad 1-q_3 \quad C_{u_1 u_2 d_3}$$
$$q_2$$
$$1-q_2 \quad C_{u_1 d_2} \quad q_3 \quad C_{u_1 d_2 u_3}$$
$$C_{u_1} \quad 1-q_3 \quad C_{u_1 d_2 d_3}$$
$$q_1$$
$$1-q_1 \quad C_{d_1} \quad C_{d_1 u_2 u_3}$$
$$q_3$$
$$C_{d_1 u_2} \quad 1-q_3 \quad C_{d_1 u_2 d_3}$$
$$q_2$$
$$1-q_2 \quad C_{d_1 d_2} \quad q_3 \quad C_{d_1 d_2 u_3}$$
$$1-q_3 \quad C_{d_1 d_2 d_3}$$

Step 1   Step 2   Step 3

the value of the firm in this step; hence, it is a riskless asset. Therefore, it should accrue at the riskless rate.

STEP 2.   Value of firm moves up by u_2 with probability q_2 or down by d_2 with probability $(1 - q_2)$. The commodity bundle accrues at the riskless rate $\hat{r}$.

STEP 3. P and V together move up by u_3 with probability q_3 or down by d_3 with probability $(1 - q_3)$.

Now folding the tree backward, one can find the expected value of the bond at node A. (See figure 5-1.) This would require knowledge of the probabilities of the upward and downward movement at each step.

Surprisingly, by creating equivalent portfolios and applying the condition that if two assets have the same value in all possible states of the world, in the next period they should have the same value as in the current period, one finds the value at node A of the bond without ever having to know the probability of upward or downward movement.

At node C, a portfolio is created that contains $\Delta \cdot u_1 \hat{r}$ of the commodity bundle and $\Delta \cdot u_2 \hat{r}$ of the firm and B risk-free bonds paying $\hat{r}$ per period. (B indicates both the risk-free bond and the quantity thereof; Δ is some number.)

Choose Δ and B such that this portfolio, if formed at C, has the same value as the commodity bond at D. That is, choose Δ and B such that $\Delta[u_1 P \hat{r} + u_2 V \hat{r}]u_3 + \hat{r}B = C_{u_1 u_2 u_3}$ where $C_{u_1 u_2 u_3}$ is the value of the bond after three steps, when the price of the commodity bundle has moved up by $u_1 u_3 \hat{r}$ and the value of the firm by $u_2 u_3 \hat{r}$. Also,

$$(5\text{-}6) \qquad \Delta[u_1 P \hat{r} + u_2 V \hat{r}]d_3 + \hat{r}B = C_{u_1 u_2 d_3}$$

We get

$$(5\text{-}7) \qquad \Delta = \frac{C_{u_1 u_2 u_3} - C_{u_1 u_2 d_3}}{(u_3 - d_3)(u_1 P \hat{r} + u_2 V \hat{r})}$$

$$(5\text{-}8) \qquad B = \frac{u_3 C_{u_1 u_2 d_3} - d_3 C_{u_1 u_2 u_3}}{(u_3 - d_3)\hat{r}}$$

If there are to be no riskless arbitrage opportunities when the bond in the next period has the same value in all states as the portfolio, the value of the bond in the present period must equal the value of the portfolio in the present period.

$$(5\text{-}9) \qquad C_{u_1 u_2} = C_{u_1 u_2} = (u_1 P \hat{r} + u_2 V \hat{r})\Delta + B$$

$$= \left[\left(\frac{\hat{r} - d_3}{u_3 - d_3} \right) C_{u_1 u_2 u_3} + \left(\frac{u_3 - \hat{r}}{u_3 - d_3} \right) C_{u_1 u_2 d_3} \right] \Big/ \hat{r}$$

Setting $P_3 = (\hat{r} - d_3/u_3 - d_3)$ and $1 - P_3 = (u_3 - \hat{r}/u_3 - d_3)$, one can write

(5-10) $$C_{u_1 u_2} = [P_3 C_{u_1 u_2 u_3} + (1 - P_3) C_{u_1 u_2 d_3}]/\hat{r}$$

Similarly all the bond values at nodes below C in figure 5-1 can be found in terms of values at the terminal nodes D. At node B, a portfolio containing Δ_1 of firm value V and B_1 risk-free bonds can be created.

Using the same procedure as above, one finds

(5-11) $$C_{u_1} = \left[\left(\frac{\hat{r} - d_2}{u_2 - d_2}\right) C_{u_1 u_2} + \left(\frac{u_2 - \hat{r}}{u_2 - d_2}\right) C_{u_1 d_2}\right] \Big/ \hat{r}$$
$$= [P_2 C_{u_1 u_2} + (1 - P_2) C_{u_1 d_2}]/\hat{r}$$

where

(5-12) $$P_2 = \left(\frac{\hat{r} - d_2}{u_2 - d_2}\right)$$

Finally, using a portfolio of Δ_2 of commodity and B_2 of bonds, one can show

(5-13) $$C = [P_1 C_{u_1} + (1 - P_1) C_{d_1}]/\hat{r}$$

where

(5-14) $$P_1 = \frac{\hat{r} - d_1}{u_1 - d_1}$$

Joined, one gets the recurrence relation for the bond value at period i in terms of the bond values at period $i + 3$.

(5-15) $$\begin{aligned} C = [&P_1 P_2 P_3 C_{u_1 u_2 u_3} + P_1 P_2 (1 - P_3) C_{u_1 u_2 d_3} \\ &+ P_1 (1 - P_2) P_3 C_{u_1 d_2 u_3} + P_1 (1 - P_2)(1 - P_3) C_{u_1 d_2 d_3} \\ &+ (1 - P_1) P_2 P_3 C_{d_1 u_2 u_3} + (1 - P_1) P_2 (1 - P_3) C_{d_1 u_2 d_3} \\ &+ (1 - P_1)(1 - P_2) P_3 C_{d_1 d_2 u_3} + (1 - P_1)(1 - P_2) \\ &\cdot (1 - P_3) C_{d_1 d_2 d_3}]/\hat{r}^3 \end{aligned}$$

where

(5-16) $$C_{u_1 u_2 u_3} = \min [u_2 u_3 \hat{r} V, F + \max (u_1 u_3 \hat{r} P - E, 0)]$$

The formula for the bond price after $3n$ periods is derived below.

(5-17) $C = \hat{r}^{-3n}\left\{\sum_{i=0}^{n}\sum_{j=0}^{n}\sum_{k=0}^{n}\left(\dfrac{n!}{i!(n-i)!}\,P_1{}^i(1-P_1)^{n-i}\right)*\right.$

$\left(\dfrac{n!}{j!(n-j)!}\,P_2{}^i(1-P_2)^{n-j}\right)*\left(\dfrac{n!}{k!(n-k)!}\,P_3^k(1-P_3)^{n-k}\right)*$

$\left. \min\,[u_2^j u_3^k d_2^{n-j} d_3^{n-k}\hat{r}^n V,\ F + \max\,(0,\ u_1^i u_3^k d_1^{n-i} d_3^{n-k}\hat{r}P - E)] \right\}$

Parameter Determination

Having derived the recurrence relation for the value of the bond after the three-step process—and thus the bond price after n in such three-step sequences—one must discover how the parameters can be derived from the observed variables.

After $3n$ periods, assuming that there are i steps for process P alone and j steps for process V alone and k steps jointly:

(5-18) $P^* = u_1^i \cdot d_1^{n-i} \cdot u_3^k d_3^{n-k} P \hat{r}^n$

(5-19) $\log\left(\dfrac{P^*}{P}\right) = i \log\dfrac{u_1}{d_1} + n \log d_1 + k \log\dfrac{u_3}{d_3} + n \log d_3 + n \log \hat{r}$

(5-20) $E\left[\log\left(\dfrac{P^*}{P}\right)\right] = E[i]\log\left(\dfrac{u_1}{d_1}\right) + E[k]\log\left(\dfrac{u_3}{d_3}\right) + n \log d_1 d_3 \hat{r}$

(5-21) $E\left[\log\left(\dfrac{P^*}{P}\right)\right] = \left[q_1 \log\left(\dfrac{u_1}{d_1}\right) + q_3\log\left(\dfrac{u_3}{d_3}\right) + \log d_1 d_3 \hat{r}\right] n$

(5-22) $\mathrm{var}\left[\log\left(\dfrac{P^*}{P}\right)\right] = \mathrm{var}\,i\left[\log\dfrac{u_1}{d_1}\right]^2 + \mathrm{var}\,k\left[\log\dfrac{u_3}{d_3}\right]^2$

$+ 2\,\mathrm{cov}\,[i, k]\log\left[\dfrac{u_1}{d_1}\right]\log\left[\dfrac{u_3}{d_3}\right]$

$= nq_1(1-q_1)\left[\log\dfrac{u_1}{d_1}\right]^2 + nq_3(1-q_3)$

$\cdot \left[\log\dfrac{u_3}{d_3}\right]^2$

(As covariance, $(i, k) = 0$ because the two steps are independent.)

Similarly, the mean and the variance for the return on V at the end of the third step can be found by substituting u_2 and d_2 for u_1 and d_1 and q_2 for q_1 in the above equations.

Finally, to find the covariance term,

$$(5\text{-}23) \quad \text{Covariance}\left\{\log\left(\frac{P^*}{P}\right), \log\left(\frac{V^*}{V}\right)\right\} = E\left\{\log\left(\frac{P^*}{P}\right)\log\left(\frac{V^*}{V}\right)\right.$$
$$\left. -E\left[\log\left(\frac{P^*}{P}\right)\right]E\left[\log\left(\frac{V^*}{V}\right)\right]\right\}$$

After substituting and then taking expectations (and sparing some tedious algebra), one gets:

$$(5\text{-}24) \qquad = [k^2 - (nq_3)^2]\left[\log\left[\frac{u_3}{d_3}\right]\right]^2$$

$$= \text{variance } [k]\left[\log\left[\frac{u_3}{d_3}\right]\right]^2$$

$$= nq_3(1 - q_3)\left[\log\left(\frac{u_3}{d_3}\right)\right]^2$$

For the covariance of the binomial process to equal the covariance of the continuous-time process, in the limit is designated as $n \to \infty$

$$(5\text{-}25) \quad \text{cov}\left[\log\left(\frac{P^*}{P}\right), \log\left(\frac{V^*}{V}\right)\right] = nq_3(1 - q_3)\left[\log\left(\frac{u_3}{d_3}\right)\right]^2 = \sigma_{pv}t$$

Further, for the means to be equal:

$$(5\text{-}26) \qquad \left[q_3 \log\left(\frac{u_3}{d_3}\right) + \log d_3\right]n = \mu_3 t$$

where σ_{pv} is the covariance and μ_3 is the mean contributed by the third process, t is the time left for maturity of the bond, and $3n$ is the total number of steps. (Because there is no real equivalent of μ_3, it is set as equal to $\mu_v - r/3$.) Setting the values of the other parameters at (reasons for specific values for parameters can be clearly seen in appendix 5-2)

$$(5\text{-}27) \qquad q_3 = \frac{1}{2} + \frac{1}{2}\left(\frac{\mu_3}{\sigma_{pv}\frac{1}{2}}\right)\sqrt{t/n}$$

and

$$(5\text{-}28) \qquad u_3 = e + \sqrt{\frac{\sigma_{pv}t}{n}} \quad d_3 = e - \sqrt{\frac{\sigma_{pv}t}{n}}$$

the covariance is provided by the third step

$$(5\text{-}29) \qquad \hat{\sigma}_{pv}n = \left[\sigma_{pv} - \mu_3\left(\frac{t}{n}\right)\right]t$$

that in the limit tends to the required value

(5-30) $\qquad \hat{\sigma}_{pv} n \to \sigma_{pv} t \quad$ as $\quad n \to \infty$

For the other two binomial processes, include

(5-31) $\qquad n \left\{ q_1(1 - q_1)\left[\log\left(\frac{u_1}{d_1}\right)\right]^2 + q_3(1 - q_3)\left[\log\left(\frac{u_3}{d_3}\right)\right]^2 \right\}$

$$= \sigma_p^2 t$$

Or in the limit as $n \to \infty$

(5-32) $\qquad n \left[q_1(1 - q_1)\left(\log\left(\frac{u_1}{d_1}\right)\right)^2 \right] = [\sigma_p^2 - \sigma_{pv}] t$

Similarly,

(5-33) $\qquad n \left[q_2(1 - q_2)\left[\log\left(\frac{u_2}{d_2}\right)\right]^2 \right] = [\sigma_v^2 - \sigma_{pv}] t$

For the means of the distributions to be equal it requires that

(5-34) $\qquad \lim_{n \to \infty} \left[q_1 \log\left(\frac{u_1}{d_1}\right) + q_3 \log\left(\frac{u_3}{d_3}\right) + \log d_1 d_3 \hat{r} \right] n = \mu_p t$

and similarly for $\mu_v t$.

The discount rate per period $\hat{r}$ should satisfy $\hat{r}^{3n} = e^{rt}$ where r is the annualized risk-free rate and t the time to maturity in years. By setting

(5-35) $\qquad u_1 = e^{+(\sqrt{\sigma_p^2 - \sigma_{pv}})\sqrt{\frac{t}{n}}} \qquad d_1 = e^{-(\sqrt{\sigma_p^2 - \sigma_{pv}})\sqrt{\frac{t}{n}}}$

(5-36) $\qquad q_1 = \frac{1}{2}\left[1 + \frac{(\mu_p - (\mu_3 + r/3))}{\sqrt{(\sigma_p^2 - \sigma_{pv})}}\sqrt{\left(\frac{t}{n}\right)} \right]$

(5-37) $\qquad u_2 = e^{\sqrt{(\sigma_v^2 - \sigma_{pv})}\sqrt{\frac{t}{n}}} \qquad d_2 = e^{-\sqrt{(\sigma_v^2 - \sigma_{pv})}\sqrt{\frac{t}{n}}}$

and

(5-38) $\qquad q_2 = \frac{1}{2}\left[1 + \frac{(\mu_v - (\mu_3 + r/3))}{\sqrt{(\sigma_v^2 - \sigma_{pv})}}\sqrt{\left(\frac{t}{n}\right)} \right],$

the required values hold in the limit.

Note that μ_3 is arbitrary, and q_1 and q_2 play no part in the valuation of the bond except to reassure that the processes are identical. So far, all that is assured is that the means and the variances of the binomial process can be made to tend to the required values. In appendix 5-2, it is demonstrated that the process tends in the limit to the same probability distribution as the bivariate normal.

Extensions

(1) *Payouts by firm.* If δ is the fraction of firm value paid out as dividend every year, it can be incorporated by diminishing the firm value every n/t iterations by δV. Bankruptcy would not occur as the value of the firm could never go to zero as a result of a fractional payout.

(2) *Coupon payments on bond.* If C is the yearly fixed coupon payment on the bond, it could be depicted by diminishing the value of the firm every n/t periods by C (and checking for default). The net coupon (after default) could be added to the bond value at that node, and the standard process could be followed to evaluate the bond value.

(3) *Stochastic interest rate.* This could be incorporated by having a fourth step (plus more for covariance terms).

(4) *Senior debt.* Senior debt could be incorporated by changing the terminal conditions: That is, if S be the amount of senior debt, the bond value at maturity

(5-39) $= \text{Min} [V - S, F + \max [0, P - E]]$

(5) *Convenience yield.* Convenience yield on the commodity option can be treated in the same way as dividends on a stock option (Fall, 1986). If C_1 is the convenience yield per period, it diminishes the value of the commodity price by $(1 - C_1)$ every period.

(6) *Terminal conditions.* Different terminal conditions could be incorporated by merely changing the function that describes the bond value on terminal date. Nothing else will have to change. Hence, an Indexed Commodity Option Note, which has a sliding stream of payments on maturity date with the underlying amount itself being a function of the price, can easily be priced. Pricing a cap is a trivial extension.

Comparative Analysis of Binomial Model and Schwartz Model Results

The model described earlier was programmed using Turbo Basic on an International Business Machines (IBM) AT personal computer (PC). First, the case assumed by Schwartz was used as a check. The extensions possible with this model were then incorporated and priced. Checks were made by taking extreme cases in which the expected result is known.

The basic case assumed by Schwartz is that of a company having issued a zero coupon with face value $F = 100$, maturing in five years. At maturity date, the bondholder has the right to buy a certain commodity bundle with initial value P and price volatility σ_v and is correlated with the commodity price movement with correlation coefficient ρ.

Table 5-1 *Commodity-Linked Bond Values for Different Commodity Bundle Prices, Firm Values, and Correlations Using the Binomial Pricing Model*
($E = F = 100, r = 0.12, T = 5.0, \sigma_p = 0.4, \sigma_v = 0.3$, number of iterations $N = 10$)

Commodity price	Pricing model	ρ			Default free
		0.0	0.35	0.70	
Firm value, V = 200					
P = 100	Binomial	86.22	93.59	103.19	
	Schwartz	85.45	93.34	102.54	
	Difference (%)	0.90	0.27	0.63	
P = 80	Binomial	77.48	83.46	89.46	
	Schwartz	77.34	83.20	89.26	
	Difference (%)	0.18	0.31	0.22	
P = 50	Binomial	65.38	67.83	69.76	
	Schwartz	65.01	67.67	69.62	
	Difference (%)	0.57	0.24	0.20	
Firm value, V = 400					
P = 100	Binomial	99.89	105.00	109.16	
	Schwartz	99.00	104.66	108.70	
	Difference (%)	0.90	0.32	0.42	
P = 80	Binomial	86.88	90.53	92.30	
	Schwartz	86.57	90.02	92.35	
	Difference (%)	0.36	0.57	−0.05	
P = 50	Binomial	69.30	70.22	70.59	
	Schwartz	68.89	70.14	70.58	
	Difference (%)	0.60	0.11	0.01	
Firm value, V = 1,000					
P = 100	Binomial	107.95	109.08	109.58	109.41
	Schwartz	107.15	108.92	109.40	109.41
	Difference (%)	0.75	0.15	0.16	0.00
P = 80	Binomial	91.59	92.50	92.42	92.42
	Schwartz	91.45	92.41	92.60	92.60
	Difference (%)	0.15	0.10	−0.20	−0.19
P = 50	Binomial	70.64	70.58	70.61	70.61
	Schwartz	70.39	70.61	70.64	70.64
	Difference (%)	0.36	−0.04	−0.04	−0.04

Table 5-1 shows the price of the bond for various values of the covariance between the commodity price and the value of the firm, as well as various values of the firm and the commodity bundle. The average difference in the prices obtained from the two models is about 0.3 percent with the maximum being 0.9 percent and the minimum being 0. This is after 10 iterations of the binomial model. In the limit, the binomial model tends toward the Schwartz model. The advantage is not just simplicity: The binomial method enables the incorporation of senior debt, payouts by the firm before the maturity of the bond (in terms of coupons and dividends), interim coupons or options linked to the commodity bond and the risk of default thereof, stochastic interest rates, caps, and others. This can be done in a simple and intuitive manner, which is important because few bonds are identically structured. Deriving the corresponding differential equation as well as solving it, even if computationally feasible, may be uneconomical. The following observations can be made from the results in table 5-1.

(1) *Effect of correlation between commodity bundle price and firm value.* The greater the correlation, the less is the risk of default and, hence, the greater the bond value. The intuition is plain; if the correlation is higher, the chances are that when the bond payments are higher because of a high commodity price, the firm value will also be higher, so that it will be able to repay without defaulting.

(2) *Effect of firm value.* The higher the firm value compared to the face value of the bond and the commodity bundle, the less the risk of default and, hence, the greater the bond value. As the firm value becomes very high compared with the potential bond obligations, however, the risk of default approaches an asymptotic limit—the default-free bond value.

(3) *Effect of higher commodity bundle price as compared to the exercise price.* The greater this difference, the higher the bond value. If the price rises so high that the firm will default continuously, however, then the bond will assume a value approaching the expected value of the firm's assets.

(4) *Effect of senior debt.* The existence of senior debt diminishes the value of the bond as the default risk goes up. The higher the value of the firm, the lower the effect of senior debt on the bond value. (See table 5-2.) Also, the higher the correlation between firm value and commodity price, the less the effect of senior debt. Note that when senior debt is referred to, it means the senior debt that matures at the same time as the bond. Any debt maturing earlier is taken as a payout by the firm.

(5) *Effect of cap.* A cap is equivalent to a call option bought by the issuer from the buyer. Thus, the bond value should be diminished by the value of the call option with exercise price equal to the cap. In table 5-3,

Table 5-2 *Effect of Senior Debt (S) on Firm Value (V)*

Correlation coefficient	V = 200			V = 400		
	S = 0	S = 100	Difference (percent)	S = 0	S = 100	Difference (percent)
$\rho = 0.35$	93.59	76.25	18.50	105.00	100.65	4.14
$\rho = 0.7$	103.19	88.28	14.40	109.16	107.29	1.70

Table 5-3 *Effect of a Commodity Price Cap on the Commodity Bond Value*

Firm value (V)	Case A (with cap = 105)	Case B (no cap)	Case C
200	66.97	93.59	26.62
400	68.32	105.00	36.68
1,000	68.40	109.08	40.38

Note: Black-Scholes value of cap = 39.74.

however, the value is not diminished by the full value of the option. This is because the issuer would not pay for the high commodity price status when bankruptcy is declared. Therefore, an increase in the risk of default on the bond would decrease the value of a cap. In the limit, a cap would have no value if the bond always defaulted and paid nothing, although it would equal the value of the option if there was no default risk.

Now, in moving beyond the Schwartz model, additions are made that are permitted by the binomial model. The starting point will be the basic bond, and features will be added so that each feature's effect on the price of the bond can be seen. The following assumptions are made:

Face value $= F = 100$ Time to maturity $= 4$ years
Exercise price $= 100$ Initial commodity price $= 100$
Coupon $= 100$ $\sigma_p = 0.4$
$\sigma_v = 0.3$ $\rho = 0.7$
Risk-free rate $= 0.12$

No default risk is assumed initially.

Table 5-4 shows that a coupon adds value to the bond, and convenience yield diminishes the value of the bond. A cap, in the absence of default risk, reduces the value of the bond by the value of an option with

Table 5-4 *Impact of Additional Features on Bond Value*

	Bond value	Incremental value
Original bond	110.62	
Additional features		
Coupon at 10 percent	140.52	29.90
Convenience yield at 5 percent	124.94	−15.58
Cap at 150	103.34	−21.60
Default risk ($v = 200$)	100.70	−2.64
Senior debt (=50)	93.46	−7.24
Payout ratio (1.0) of firm	80.45	−13.01

exercise price equal to the cap. (The value of the cap is estimated at 21.28 in the Black formula as compared with 21.60 here.) Increased payout and senior debt have no effect if default risk is not considered. In the presence of default risk, however, senior debt diminishes the value of the bond, as do payouts to equity or other bonds. The cap, however, will be worth less.

Some Comparative Statics

The various parameters will be now varied for the bond above, and the values of the zero-bond (principal and option repayment) and coupons will be established.

The effects of varying are as follows:

(1) *Firm value.* Coupons are paid whenever they are due. Therefore, the default on the coupon is only likely when the firm value is comparable to the size of coupon payments. This can be seen in figure 5-2 where default on the coupon starts only when the initial firm value is below 50. Above 50, however, the coupon is not defaulted on and maintains a constant value. Similarly, default on the principal and option repayment becomes negligible at a firm value higher than 600.

Figure 5-2 *Bond Values for Different Firm Values*

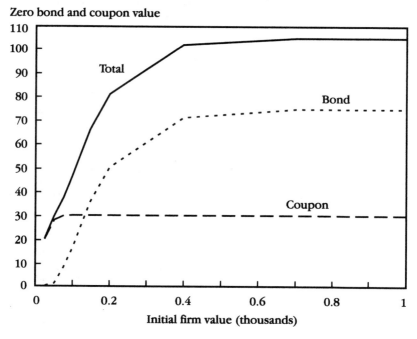

Figure 5-3 *Bond Values for Different Coupon Rates*

Zero bond and coupon value

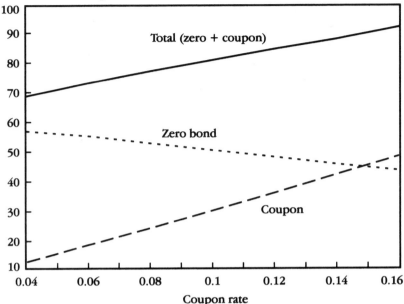

(2) *Coupon rates.* Higher coupon rates increase the present value of the coupon, but simultaneously decrease the value of the zero bond. (See figure 5-3.) This is because a higher coupon diminishes the value of the firm more and leaves a lower amount to repay the principal/option. The net effect is that a higher coupon does not increase the value of the bond as much in the presence of default risk as it would a default-free bond.

(3) *Convenience yields.* The effect of convenience yields is important as these are fairly volatile for some commodities, such as oil. From figure 5-4, it can be seen that a sharp change in convenience yields, for example, from 20 to −20 percent, changes the total bond value by about 10 percent.

(4) *Senior debt.* Here, senior debt refers to debt maturing at the same time as the bond, but being senior to the bond. The larger the senior debt, the greater the chance of default on the principal/option, as seen in figure 5-5. Dividend or other payouts earlier than the bond maturity have a similar effect. (See figure 5-6).

(5) *Caps.* Caps are effective as long as they are at price levels that have high probabilities of being attained; at higher levels, they are of negligible value. (See figure 5-7.)

Figure 5-4 *Bond Values for Different Convenience Yields*

Zero bond and coupon value

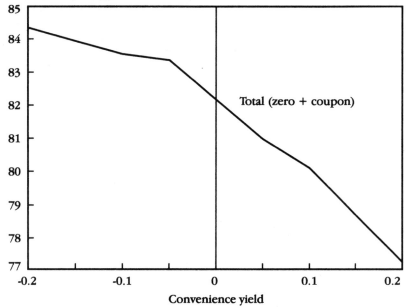

Convenience yield

Figure 5-5 *Bond Values for Different Senior Debt Amounts*

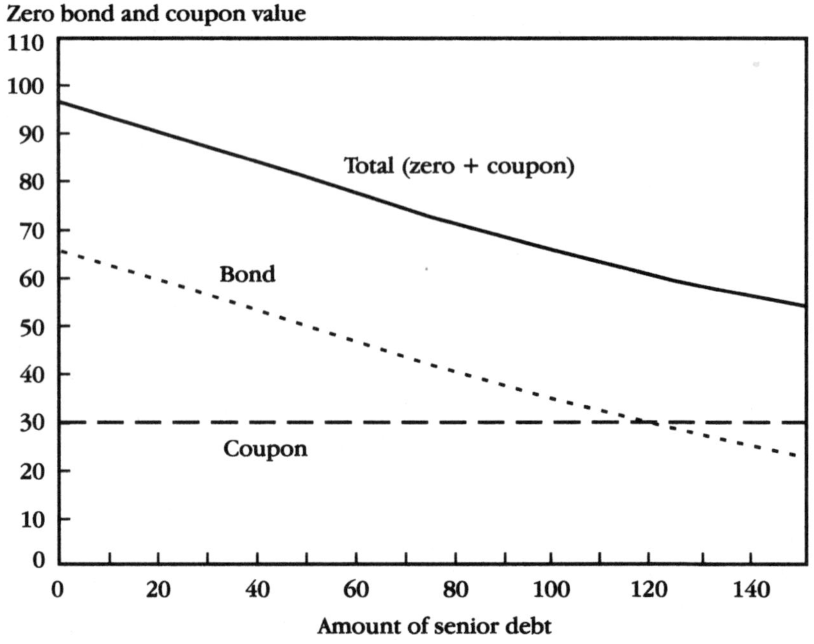

Zero bond and coupon value

Figure 5-6 *Bond Values for Different Payout Ratios*

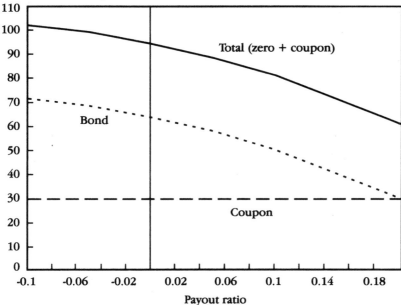

Figure 5-7 *Bond Values for Different Caps*

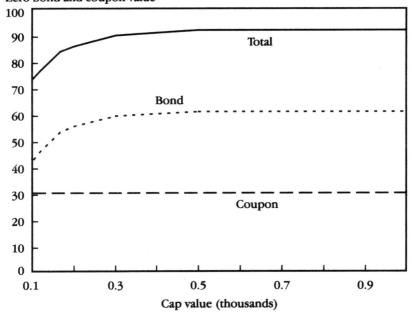

Figure 5-8 *Bond Values for Different Correlations*

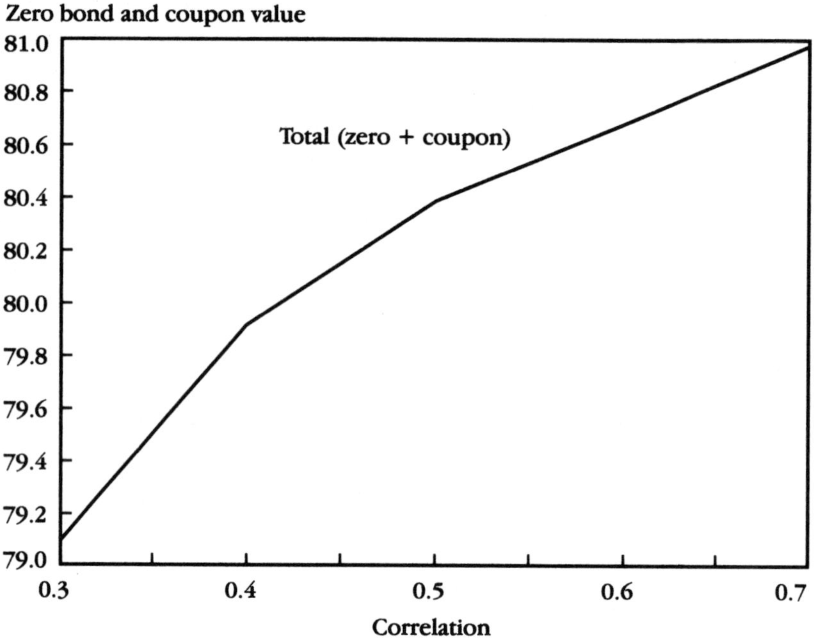

Zero bond and coupon value

(6) *Correlation*. Correlation between the firm value and the commodity bundle price decreases the default risk and, hence, the value of the bond. (See figure 5-8.)

Conclusion

The binomial model is an effective way of pricing a commodity bond in the presence of commodity price risk and default risk. Extensions to incorporate other sources of risk can be made easily. The limiting factor in all this is computational power, but it becomes significant only in the presence of features like fixed coupon payments or fixed payouts.

The application of this intuitive method to commodity-linked bonds is just one of the many applications possible. For example, secondary market developing country debt could be priced by suitably redefining V (the value of the firm) and P (the price of the commodity).

Appendix 5-1. The Continuous-Time Model

Using the traditional continuous-time option pricing method, it can be shown that if the price of the commodity bundle P and the value of the firm V follow stochastic processes:

$$(5\text{-}40) \qquad \frac{dP}{P} = \mu_p dt + \sigma_p dZp$$

$$(5\text{-}41) \qquad \frac{dV}{V} = \mu_v dt + \sigma_v dZv$$

and

$$(5\text{-}42) \qquad dZ_p dZ_v = \sigma_{pv} dt$$

the differential equation to be solved is

$$(5\text{-}43) \qquad \frac{1}{2}\sigma_p^2 P^2 B_{pp} + \frac{1}{2}\sigma_v^2 V^2 B_{vv} + \sigma_{pv} PV B_{pv}$$
$$+ PB_p(r - \delta) + B_v[rV - D] - B_z - rB + C = 0$$

where B is the value of the bond, Z is the time to expiration, δ is the convenience yield, D is the total payout by firm per year, and C is the yearly coupon attached to the bond.
The boundary conditions are:

$$(5\text{-}44) \qquad B(P, V, 0) = \min [V, F + \max (0, P - E)]$$

where F is the face value of the bond.

If payout D is assumed to be a fixed fraction d of the firm value V and the coupon C is a fixed fraction c of the face value of the bond, default must be checked every time the coupon is paid; that is, $V \geq C$.

The solution to this equation (if at all possible) would be very cumbersome, even by most numerical methods.

Appendix 5-2. Proof That the Distribution of the Binomial Model Tends to the Bivariate Normal Distribution

To show that the binomial model tends in the limit to the bivariate normal distribution, the characteristic function of the former is shown to tend toward the latter.

Consider the three-step process in figure 5-1. There are eight terminal nodes at D that are numbered from top to bottom 1 to 8. At the top-most node, the commodity price is $Pu_1 u_3 r$. Therefore, the log of the return on the commodity over the three steps at node 1 is

$$(5\text{-}45) \qquad \log R_1 = \log u_1 + \log u_3 + \log \hat{r}$$

Similarly, the log return on the firm is

(5-46) $\log R_2 = \log u_2 + \log u_3 + \log \hat{r}$

To determine the characteristic function of joint returns (log R_1, log R_2), denoted as $\phi(\theta_1, \theta_2)$

(5-47) $\phi(\theta_1, \theta_2) = E\left[\exp\left(i\theta_1 \log R_1, i\theta_2 \log R_2\right)\right]$

The expectation over the three-step process is the sum of eight terms, each arising from a particular outcome of (log R_1, log R_2)

(5-48) $$\phi(\theta_1, \theta_2) = \sum_{i=1}^{8} D_i$$

where

(5-49) $D_1 = q_1 q_2 q_3 \exp\left[i\theta_1(\log u_1 + \log u_3 + \log \hat{r})\right.$

$\left. + i\theta_2(\log u_2 + \log u_3 + \log \hat{r})\right]$

$= \dfrac{q_1 q_2}{2} \dfrac{\left[1 + \mu_3 \sqrt{h}\right]}{\sigma_3} \exp\left[i\theta_1(\sigma_3\sqrt{h} + \sigma_a\sqrt{h} + \log rt/3n)\right.$

$\left. + i\theta_2(\sigma_3\sqrt{h} + \sigma_b\sqrt{h} + \log rt/3n)\right]$

where $h = t/n, \sigma_3 = \sqrt{\sigma_{pv}}, \sigma_a = \sqrt{(\sigma_p^2 - \sigma_{pv})}, \sigma_b = \sqrt{(\sigma_v^2 - \sigma_{pv})}$

(5-50) $D_1 = \dfrac{q_1 q_2}{2} \dfrac{\{1 + \mu_3\sqrt{h}\}}{\sigma_3} \exp\left\{\sqrt{h}[i\theta_1(\sigma_3 + \sigma_a)\right.$

$\left. + i\theta_2(\sigma_3 + \sigma_b)] + h[i\theta_1 r/3 + i\theta_2 r/3]\right\}$

Expanding the exponential as a power series, multiplying out, and rearranging, one gets:

(5-51)

$$D_1 = \frac{q_1 q_2}{2}\left\{1 + \sqrt{h}\left[\frac{\mu_3}{\sigma_3} + i\theta_1(\sigma_3 + \sigma_a) + i\theta_2(\sigma_3 + \sigma_b)\right]\right.$$

$$+ h\left[\frac{\mu_3}{\sigma_3} i\theta_1(\sigma_3 + \sigma_a) + \frac{\mu_3}{\sigma_3} i\theta_2(\sigma_3 + \sigma_b)\right.$$

$$+ i\theta_1 r/3 + i\theta_2 r/3 - \frac{\theta_1^2}{2}(\sigma_3 + \sigma_a)^2$$

$$\left.\left. - \theta_1\theta_2(\sigma_3 + \sigma_a)(\sigma_3 + \sigma_b) - \frac{\theta_2^2}{2}(\sigma_3 + \sigma_b)^2\right] + o(h)\right\}$$

where $o(h)$ indicates power of h higher than 1, which will be negligible in the limit.

Summing over all the eight nodes (i.e., finding the corresponding expression to D_1 above one for $D_2:D_8$ and then adding them all together), a tedious but necessary process, and then simplifying, one gets:

$$(5\text{-}52) \quad \phi(\theta_1,\theta_2) = 1 + \sqrt{h}[i\theta_1\sigma_a(2q_1 - 1) + i\theta_2\sigma_b(2q_2 - 1)] +$$

$$+ h\Bigg[i\theta_1\mu_3 + i\theta_2\mu_3 + i\theta_1 r/3 + i\theta_2 r/3 + \frac{\theta_1^2}{2}(\sigma_3^2 + \sigma_a^2)$$

$$+ \frac{\theta_2^2}{2}(\sigma_3^2 + \sigma_b^2) + \theta_1\theta_2(\sigma_3^2)$$

$$+ (2q_1 - 1)(2q_2 - 1)\sigma_a\sigma_b\Bigg] + o(h)$$

Setting

$$q_1 = \frac{1}{2}\Bigg[1 + \Bigg(\mu_p - \frac{(\mu_3 + r/3)}{\sigma_a}\Bigg)\sqrt{\Bigg(\frac{t}{n}\Bigg)}\Bigg], \quad q_2 = \frac{1}{2} \text{ and } \mu_3 = \mu_v - r/3$$

and substituting back for σ_a, σ_b, σ_3 one gets:

$$(5\text{-}53) \qquad \phi(\theta_1, \theta_2) = 1 + h\{[i\theta_1\mu_1 + i\theta_2\mu_2]$$

$$- \frac{1}{2}[\theta_1^2\sigma_p^2 + \theta_2^2\sigma_v^2 + 2\theta_1\theta_2\sigma_{pv}]\} + o(h)$$

After n such sequences, it is known that

$$(5\text{-}54) \qquad \phi_n(\theta_1,\theta_2) = [\phi(\theta_1,\theta_2)]^n$$

occurs from the independence of successive processes. Therefore, allowing $n \to \infty$ such that $h = t/n \to 0$, one gets

$$(5\text{-}55)$$

$$\lim_{n\to\infty} \phi_n(\theta_1,\theta_2) = 1 + t\Bigg\{i\theta_1\mu_p + i\theta_2\mu_v - \frac{1}{2}(\theta_1^2\sigma_p^2 + \theta_2^2\sigma_v^2 + 2\theta_1\theta_2\sigma_{pv})\Bigg\}$$

But the characteristic function for the joint lognormal diffusion process with parameters μ_p, μ_v, σ_p, σ_v is

$$(5\text{-}56)$$

$$\psi(\theta_1,\theta_2) = 1 + (i\theta_1\mu_1 t + i\theta_2\mu_2 t) - \frac{1}{2}(\theta_1^2\sigma_p^2 t + \theta_2^2\sigma_v^2 t + 2\theta_1\theta_2\sigma_{pv}t)$$

that is the limit of the binomial.

Notes

1. All starred (*) terms are values on the date of maturity.

2. The European option differs from an American one in that it can be exercised only upon expiration, rather than at any time.

3. This is not the case for a sovereign issue. In a developing country, when a corporate bondholder defaults, government authorities often assume foreign obligations.

4. See Cox, Ross, and Rubenstein (1979).

PART II

Commodity Contingency in the International Lending of Developing Countries

6

Optimal External Debt Management with Commodity-Linked Bonds

Robert J. Myers and Stanley R. Thompson

Much of the spectacular growth in external borrowing by developing countries that occurred during the 1970s was in the form of general obligation loans denominated in U.S. dollars at floating interest rates. It is now well understood that this strategy involved substantial risks in respect to exchange rates, interest rates, and commodity prices. These risks became all too clear following the developing country debt crisis that began in 1982. The deterioration in the developing countries' terms of trade quickly eroded their ability to service their burgeoning debts. In turn, this led to restricted access to new external credit and a period of forced adjustment in consumption and investment. A disturbing number of heavily indebted countries have not yet emerged from the resulting difficulties.

This chapter examines the way in which commodity-linked bonds could be used by developing countries to hedge the risks associated with their external debt position. Commodity-linked bonds are bonds that have principal, and possibly coupon payments, linked to future realizations of a specified set of commodity prices. By issuing bonds linked to the prices of commodities that they export, developing countries would be hedging against the risk of a deterioration in export earnings because of a fall in these prices. If developing country debt had been issued in the form of commodity-linked bonds, debt service obligations would have fallen along with commodity prices, thus easing the burden of adjusting to the external shock. Of course, other commodity-linked financial instruments, such as futures and options contracts, could be used for similar hedging purposes. Futures and options, however, do not exist for many commodities and typically have only short maturities. Thus, for many developing countries, commodity-linked bonds show considerable potential as a financial risk management instrument.

The characteristics of alternative international financial instruments, including commodity-linked bonds, have been discussed extensively elsewhere. (See Lessard, 1977a; Lessard and Williamson, 1985; and O'Hara, 1984.) The specific purpose here is to provide an operational rule for choosing an optimal external debt portfolio consisting of commodity-linked bonds and conventional debt. To begin, a simple dynamic model is used to derive optimal rules for issuing commodity-linked bonds and conventional debt in a small, open economy. Next, estimation methods that allow these rules to be operationalized are presented. The approach is then illustrated with an application to Costa Rica, where the optimal external debt portfolio would contain a significant proportion of commodity-linked bonds.

A Model of Optimal External Debt Allocation

Consider a small, open economy in which all external debt is issued by the government. The government has a utility function, $u(m_t)$, defined over real imports of goods and services per capita in period t. This utility function is meant to capture the contribution that imports make to domestic consumption and growth. It satisfies the von Neumann-Morgenstern axioms, as well as the conditions $u'(m_t) > 0$ and $u''(m_t) < 0$. Commodity exports by the country are assumed to follow an exogenous stochastic process that is not influenced by the government's external debt decisions. Real exports per capita in period t are denoted x_t.

Without external finance, the value of imports must equal the value of exports so that the current account is in balance each period. It is assumed, however, that the government has access to two sources of external finance. First, it can take out conventional loans at the constant real interest rate r. Real total debt per capita held in the form of conventional loans at the end of period t is denoted d_t. Second, the government can issue bonds linked to each of n commodities. When issued, these bonds have real prices $w_t = (w_{1t}, w_{2t}, \ldots, w_{nt})$ and the real prices of the underlying commodities are denoted $p_t = (p_{1t}, p_{2t}, \ldots, p_{nt})$. Future commodity prices are stochastic when the government issues the bonds. The bonds mature in one period and require a financial payment at maturity that is equal to the price of the underlying commodity.[1] To simplify the analysis, no coupon payments on the bonds are assumed. The per capita quantity of bonds issued by the government at time t is denoted $b_t = (b_{1t}, b_{2t}, \ldots, b_{nt})'$.

With these assumptions, the constraint facing the government when it chooses an external debt portfolio is

(6-1) $\qquad m_t + rd_{t-1} + p_t b_{t-1} \leq x_t + (d_t - d_{t-1}) + w_t b_t.$

The government is also restricted in that it cannot borrow indefinitely to finance ever-increasing current account deficits. This constraint is imposed by requiring

(6-2) $\qquad \lim_{T \to \infty} d_T = \lim_{T \to \infty} b_T = 0.$

The government's problem is now to choose issues of conventional debt and commodity-linked bonds that maximize the discounted time-additive expected utility function

(6-3) $$E_0 \sum_{t=0}^{\infty} \beta^t u(m_t)$$

subject to the sequence of constraints in equation 6-1 and the transversality conditions in equation 6-2.

The solution to the government's problem must satisfy 6-1 and 6-2, plus the Euler equations

(6-4) $\qquad u'(m_t) - \beta(1+r)E_t u'(m_{t+1}) = 0$

and

(6-5) $\qquad u'(m_t)w_t - \beta E_t[u'(m_{t+1})p_{t+1}] = 0.$

Finding a closed form solution is generally impossible without placing strong restrictions on the form of the utility function and on the probability distribution of prices and exports. Here, however, in accordance with the literature on the permanent income theory of consumption, it is assumed that the optimal import path can be defined[2] as

(6-6) $\qquad m_t = \alpha\left[\sum_{i=0}^{\infty} (1+r)^{-i} E_t(x_{t+i}) - p_t b_{t-1} - (1+r)d_{t-1} \right].$

Notice that this is just a version of the permanent income theory of consumption—imports are set equal to some proportion, α, of "permanent" exports (a discounted sum of expected future export revenues, minus current external debt).

Equation 6-6 is not yet a decision rule because the terms $E_t(x_{t+i})$ must be eliminated by expressing them as a function of variables known by the government at time t. Suppose that x_t is the first element of a vector, $y_t = (x_t, p_{1t}, p_{2t}, \ldots, p_{nt}, s_t)'$, that also contains the commodity prices and any other state variables useful for predicting future exports. The vector y_t is assumed to follow the autoregressive process

(6-7) $\qquad A(L)y_t = \varepsilon_t$

where $A(L) = I - A_1L - A_2L^2 - \cdots - A_qL^q$ is a matrix polynomial in the lag operator and ε_t is a zero mean serially uncorrelated error vector with covariance matrix Ω. In the next section, it is demonstrated that optimal projections of $E_t(x_{t+1})$, given the autoregressive process 6-7 and information available at time t, lead to

$$(6\text{-}8) \qquad \sum_{i=0}^{\infty} (1 + r)^{-i} E_t(x_{t+i}) = \gamma y_t + B(L)y_{t-1}$$

for some parameter vector γ and some matrix polynomial in the lag operator $B(L)$. Both γ and $B(L)$ are defined explicitly below in the estimation section.

Substituting 6-8 in 6-6 gives the operational decision rule

$$(6\text{-}9) \qquad m_t = \alpha[\gamma y_t + B(L)y_{t-1} - p_t b_{t-1} - (1 + r)d_{t-1}].$$

Although this rule defines the optimal level of imports, and thus the optimal level of total external debt, it does not provide the optimal portfolio of commodity-linked bonds, however. To derive the optimal bond portfolio, notice that the Euler equations 6-4 and 6-5 can be substituted and rearranged to give

$$(6\text{-}10) \qquad E_t\{u'(m_{t+1})[w_t - p_{t+1}/(1 + r)]\} = 0.$$

Next, take a linear approximation of $u'(m_{t+1})$ at m_t so that this equation becomes

$$(6\text{-}11) \quad E_t\{m_{t+1}[w_t - p_{t+1}/(1 + r)]\} = m_t E_t[w_t - p_{t+1}/(1 + r)].$$

Assuming that the expected real return on holding bonds is equal to the real interest rate, $E_t[w_t + p_{t+1}/(1 + r)] = 0$, then 6-11 implies that the conditional covariance between m_{t+1} and p_{t+1} must be zero at an optimum.[3] Leading 6-9 one period and computing the relevant covariance shows that the optimal commodity-linked bond portfolio satisfies

$$(6\text{-}12) \qquad \Omega_{py}\gamma' - \Omega_{pp}b_t = 0$$

where Ω_{py} is a matrix of conditional covariances between p_{t+1} and y_{t+1}, and Ω_{pp} is the conditional covariance matrix for p_{t+1}. Solving for b_t gives

$$(6\text{-}13) \qquad b_t = \Omega_{pp}^{-1}\Omega_{py}\gamma'.$$

The per capita amount of total finance raised at time t from issuing an optimal portfolio of commodity-linked bonds can be obtained by premultiplying 6-13 by the bond prices, w_t. A method for estimating 6-13 is provided in the next section. It is interesting to note that 6-13 is precisely the solution that would be obtained from a two-period mean-variance formulation of the optimal portfolio problem, except that γ would have a one in the first column and zeros elsewhere. In the infinite horizon problem, expectations concerning export performance at *all* future dates are important, however, and the optimal portfolio must be weighted accordingly.

Estimation

Estimation of the optimal commodity-linked bond portfolio revolves around the vector autoregressive process $A(L)y_t = \varepsilon_t$, which was defined in the previous section. Remembering that y_t contains all of the commodity prices that are linked to bonds (as well as x_t and other state variables helpful in predicting future export revenues), then the conditional covariance matrices Ω_{py} and Ω_{pp} in 6-13 are clearly just components of Ω, the covariance matrix of ε_t. Thus, estimation of the vector autoregressive process for y_t will provide an estimate of Ω that, in turn, can be used directly to operationalize 6-13.

Estimation of the vector autoregressive process for y_t is also useful for another reason. To compute optimal bond issues from 6-13, one needs to know the parameter vector γ. From 6-8, recall that γ represents coefficients on y_t in the optimal prediction of a discounted sum of future realizations of export revenues, given current and past values of y_t. From a formula derived by Hansen and Sargent, this optimal predictor is

$$(6\text{-}14) \quad \sum_{i=0}^{\infty} (1 + r)^{-i} E_t(x_{t+1}) = \phi A[1/(1 + r)]^{-1} y_t + B(L)y_{t-2}$$

where ϕ is a row vector with a one in the first column and zeros elsewhere, and $B(L)$ satisfies

$$(6\text{-}15) \quad B(L) = \phi A[1/(1 + r)]^{-1} \left\{ \sum_{j=1}^{q-1} \left[\sum_{k=j+1}^{q} (1 + r)^{j-k} A^k \right] L^{j+1} \right\}.$$

Thus, γ is simply the first row of $A[1/(1 + r)]^{-1}$. Evidently, estimation of the autoregressive parameters in $A(L)$ provides a direct estimate of γ (conditional on knowledge of the real interest rate r). Actual estimation of the parameters in $A(L)$ and Ω can be accomplished via vector autoregression.[4]

The final piece of the estimation puzzle lies in obtaining an estimate of the real interest rate, r. Once r has been found, and $A(L)$ and Ω have been estimated, then computing the optimal commodity-linked bond issues is straightforward using 6-13. In many cases, prior information will be available on real interest rates. In the following application to Costa Rica, optimal external debt portfolios for a number of different real interest rates are presented, and the results indicate that they are not sensitive to this value.

The Case of Costa Rica

Costa Rica is a small country that depends on a handful of agricultural commodities for the bulk of its export earnings. In recent years, coffee, beef, and bananas have accounted for more than half of total export revenues. Figure 6-1 shows gross national product (GNP), consumption, and investment for Costa Rica between 1966 and 1986, all in real per capita terms. The pronounced slump that began around 1981 and continued into 1983 is indicative of the problems that many developing countries have experienced since the onset of the debt crisis. Figure 6-2 shows Costa Rica's terms of trade index and their total foreign debt in U.S. dollars. The data suggest that the economic slump of 1981–83 was preceded by a sharp negative terms of trade shock and a dramatic increase in debt servicing requirements. By linking debt service requirements to commodity price realizations, commodity-linked bonds might help facilitate adjustment and avoid future slumps of this severity.

Figure 6-1 *Real per Capita Gross National Product Consumption and Investment for Costa Rica, 1966-86*

1980 Colones per capita

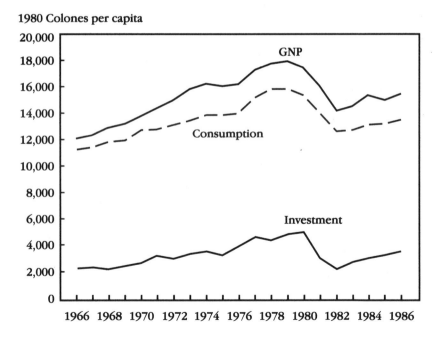

Source: **World Bank data.**

Figure 6-2 *Terms of Trade and Per Capita Total External Debt for Costa Rica, 1966-86*

Terms of trade (1980 = 100)

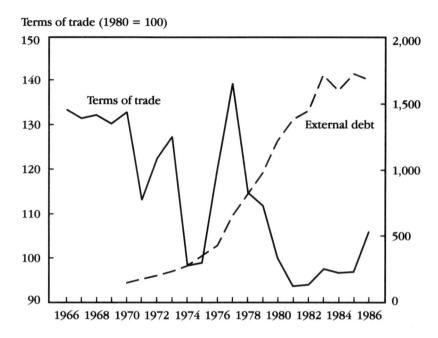

Source: World Bank data.

To illustrate the estimation of optimal external debt portfolios, a Costa Rican portfolio of conventional loans and bonds linked to three major export commodities—coffee, beef, and bananas—was examined. Real prices of these commodities are denoted p_{ct}, p_{bt}, and p_{at} respectively. The first task was to estimate the vector autoregressive process for real exports and the three real commodity prices. To simplify, the possibility of including other variables in the model was not considered. Nominal prices and nominal export revenues, all in U.S. dollars, were each deflated by an index of import prices for Costa Rica. The commodity prices were obtained from World Bank (1985), and all other data are from World Bank (1988). The data are annual, and the sample runs from 1966 through 1985.

In view of the small number of available observations, an equation-by-equation approach to model specification was used. Preliminary investigations revealed no strong evidence of nonstationarity or hetero-

Table 6-1 *Estimation Results*

$x_t = 219.55 + 0.63\ x_{t-1} - 0.11\ x_{t-2};$ $\bar{R}^2 = 0.36$
      (3.78) (4.14) (0.78)

$p_t^c = 2.82 + 0.42\ p_{t-1}^c - 0.10\ p_{t-2}^c;$ $\bar{R}^2 = 0.23$
      (3.92) (2.63) (0.65)

$p_t^b = 0.61 + 0.84\ p_{t-1}^b - 0.05\ p_{t-2}^b;$ $\bar{R}^2 = 0.57$
      (1.13) (3.87) (0.22)

$p_t^a = 0.05 + 0.48\ p_{t-1}^a + 0.65\ p_{t-2}^a - 0.04\ p_{t-1}^b;$ $\bar{R}^2 = 0.58$
      (1.12) (3.11) (3.75) (4.14)

$$\hat{\Omega} = \begin{bmatrix} 2{,}238.4 & 39.2 & 9.9 & 0.9 \\ 39.2 & 0.99 & 0.15 & 0.02 \\ 9.9 & 0.15 & 0.44 & -0.019 \\ 0.9 & 0.02 & -0.081 & 0.001 \end{bmatrix}$$

Note: Values in parentheses are *t*-values.

scedastic errors, so the models were estimated in the levels of each variable, assuming a constant conditional covariance matrix. Initially, an overfitted equation was specified with lags of all four variables included. Then F-tests were used to test zero restrictions on sets of coefficients. Estimation results for the final model specification are shown in table 6-1, where the system was estimated using seemingly unrelated regression. Table 6-1 also contains the resulting estimated conditional covariance matrix.

The optimal external debt portfolio was computed for 1985, the last year of the sample. The matrices Ω_{py} and Ω_{pp} come directly from table 6-1, and the parameter vector γ is computed from the estimates in the table (as shown above). Each optimal commodity-linked bond issue was

Table 6-2 *Optimal Portfolios in 1985 as a Proportion of Total External Debt*

r	General obligation loans	Coffee	Beef	Bananas
0.00	.655	0.144	0.035	0.166
0.05	.652	0.145	0.036	0.167
0.10	.649	0.147	0.036	0.168

multiplied by an estimate of its price. This estimate was obtained by using the vector autoregression to forecast commodity prices into 1986 (given information available in 1985) and then discounted back using the real interest rate. The final revenue figure was then expressed as a proportion of the actual level of total external debt in Costa Rica in 1985.

The estimated optimal external debt portfolio is presented in table 6-2 under three different real interest rate assumptions. Clearly, the portfolios are not very sensitive to the real interest rate used. The results suggest that more than 30 percent of total debt should be issued in the form of commodity-linked bonds, with the bulk of these issues being split between coffee and bananas. The optimal portfolio of external debt for Costa Rica in 1985, therefore, appears to contain a significant proportion of commodity-linked bonds.

Concluding Comments

This chapter provides a simple dynamic model that can be used to estimate optimal portfolios of external debt. It focuses on the potential role of commodity-linked bonds in hedging against the possibility of a deterioration in a country's terms of trade. The approach was applied to Costa Rica, where it was found that a significant proportion of external debt should be issued in the form of commodity-linked bonds.

The framework could be extended in a variety of directions. In particular, although optimal portfolios of external debt have been computed, the extent of reductions in the variance of real imports has not yet been determined. This information is critical in determining the hedging effectiveness of commodity-linked bonds. Future research might also examine expanded portfolios, perhaps looking at other commodity-linked instruments, such as futures, options, and bonds linked to indices of commodity prices.

There are a number of practical difficulties associated with commodity-linked bonds that deserve additional attention. In this paper, it has simply been assumed that markets for these instruments exist, and that such markets have no risk premia. It seems likely that commodity-linked bonds would be priced at a discount, however, especially if issued by developing countries subject to significant default risk. In fact, the size of risk premia may be an important reason why there is currently such little use made of commodity-linked bonds. Nevertheless, the analysis presented above suggests a potential hedging role for commodity-linked bonds, provided that diversified markets for these contracts can emerge and grow.

Notes

1. For simplicity, attention is restricted to bonds with a one-period maturity. An extension to longer-term maturities, however, would be relatively straightforward.

2. Assumptions sufficient to guarantee this equation is an exact solution are: (1) the expected real return to holding bonds is equal to the real interest rate $E_t[W_{t+1} - P_{t+1+i}/(1 + r) = 0$ for $i = 0, 1, \ldots$; and *either* (2) utility is quadratic *or* (3) utility features constant absolute risk aversion and m_t is normally distributed with a variance that depends only on i or (4) utility features constant relative risk aversion and log m_t is normally distributed with a variance that depends only on i. See Evans (1988) and the references therein for more details on the latter three conditions. A complete derivation of equation 6-6 under these conditions is available from the authors on request.

3. This implies that there are no risk premia in commodity-linked bond prices. If investors are risk adverse and cannot diversify all of the risks of investing in the bonds, then the bonds may be priced at a discount to conventional debt. (Schwartz, 1982)

4. No discussion of vector autoregression estimation techniques is included here. Those interested should consult Engle and Bollerslev (1986), Engle and Granger (1977), Sims (1980), and others.

7

Integrating Commodity and Exchange Rate Risk Management: Implications for External Debt Management

Stijn Claessens

> Other things being equal, a strengthening of the dollar will worsen the terms of trade of net commodity exporters and hence reduce their welfare. For net commodity importers, the reverse pattern will hold.[1]

> . . . for some countries, the fall in the dollar increased the burden of debt relative to their economies.[2]

Who is right, *ex ante* and *ex post*, about the effect of a cross-currency movement on the welfare of developing countries? Even though both quotations are, of course, deliberately placed out of context, they do illustrate some of the unresolved issues regarding the effect of cross-currency movements on the welfare of developing countries. The aim of this chapter is to at least clarify, and potentially resolve, some of these outstanding issues. Furthermore, the chapter attempts to present conceptual and practical guidelines that will help with external debt management generally.

During the past decade, many developing countries have been affected by the large volatility in cross-currency exchange rates and commodity prices as a result of the impact of these changes on the relative burden of their external debt service. Cross-currency exchange rate changes have affected the structure, as well as the level, of many developing countries' external debt. This is, for instance, demonstrated by the fact that the share of dollar-denominated debt has varied substantially in the 1980s due to large swings in the dollar vis-à-vis other lending currencies and due to the fact that a substantial part of developing countries' debt is denominated in non-U.S. dollar currencies.[3] The external debt of many developing countries as measured in U.S. dollars has thus fluctuated considerably during the 1980s as a result of movements in the dollar.[4] Commodity price movements in the 1980s have also had a dramatic impact on many developing countries' exports earnings. This is demonstrated, for instance, by the changes in the World Bank index for agricultural raw material prices, which fell from an index value of 100 in 1980 to 78 in 1985 and bounced back up to 120 in 1988.[5]

The interactions between cross-currency exchange rate fluctuations and commodity price changes—and the combined effects of the two—have affected the structure and the level of many developing countries' external debt *relative* to their debt-servicing capacity. For an example in which these two effects interacted in an adverse way, one can look to the case of Indonesia. The debt service-to-exports ratio for Indonesia rose from 8.2 percent in 1981 to 27.8 percent in 1987—an increase of which more than 65 percent can be explained by the depreciation of the U.S. dollar since 1985 and the fall in oil and other commodity prices since 1986. As a further example, rough calculations indicate that if commodity prices and exchange rates had remained at their end-of-1982 values, and assuming no reduction or increase in financial flows, the debt service-to-exports ratio for all developing countries would have been approximately 17 percent in 1987 in contrast to the actual level of 24 percent.

Entities in developed countries are able to hedge against exchange rate changes by purchasing currency futures or other short-term hedging instruments on organized or over-the-counter markets. They can also hedge against commodity price movements by buying commodity hedging instruments. Most developing countries, however, do not have sufficient access to these markets because of institutional and credit constraints, as well as for other reasons.

An alternative hedging instrument that can be used to reduce the impact of the combined effect of cross-currency exchange *and* commodity price uncertainty, and that is more likely available to a larger group of developing countries, is the currency composition of external debt. Developing countries (or agents within these countries) can minimize their vulnerability to the combined effects of currency and commodity price risks by optimizing the currency composition of their external debt with respect to established relationships between (lenders') exchange rates and the cash flows with which they service their debt (i.e., export earnings). Even though an optimal currency composition of external debt might be difficult to attain for some developing countries—because they might be constrained in choosing and altering the currency composition of their new and existing borrowings (such as in the case of bilateral loans from foreign governments) and because they might not be able to use long-term financial market hedging techniques, such as currency swaps, to alter the currency composition of their existing debt—knowing what the optimal currency composition of external debt would be and what (marginal) changes are required to achieve such a composition will still lead to substantial benefits in terms of reducing the vulnerability of their economies to exchange rate and commodity price uncertainty.

Ex post, one could determine an optimal portfolio in terms of currency composition; however, this does not necessarily help in developing policy rules on the way in which developing countries can minimize their vulnerability to exchange risks and commodity price risks *ex ante*. The *ex ante* problem has not been given much attention in the analytical literature, and only a few empirical applications of optimal currency composition of external debt exist. The purpose of this chapter is, therefore, first to review all the existing, mostly policy-oriented literature and suggestions as to the way in which external debt should be allocated across different currencies. Second, this chapter will discuss the weaknesses of these guidelines. Then, a theoretical model of optimal currency composition is presented, which is an abbreviated version of the model given in Claessens (1988). Some empirical results for Indonesia and Turkey, derived on the basis of this theoretical model, are then summarized. These were reported in earlier work (Kroner and Claessens, 1988).

Issues in Joint Commodity and Exchange Risk Management

Diversification

Before discussing some of the issues regarding the hedging potential of the currency composition of (long-term) external liabilities, one should note that there are other options open to a country to reduce its exposure to external factors. First, the country can engage in real diversification through the sourcing, producing, and exporting of a mix of products that is close to optimal, given the relationships between exchange rates, goods' prices, and other external factors. Of course, the composition of exports and, to a lesser extent, of imports cannot be changed easily in the short run, but one can expect significant contributions from closer-to-optimal real activity diversification in the long run. Second, a range of instruments is available to private firms in developed financial markets to manage short-term exposures, and some of these instruments could be used to manage a country's external exposures. Transfer of certain risks to market participants more able to absorb them, or able to transfer these risks to others, can substantially benefit a developing country by reducing risks at reasonable costs.[6]

Real activity diversification and use of short-term hedging instruments, however, might leave little room for hedging because the country is likely to be constrained in the short term (and the long term) on the real side and may not have access to (short-term) financial hedging instruments. The country might, therefore, want to use the currency composition of new external capital flows as a hedging instrument against unanticipated exchange rate and commodity price movements. In addition, the country might want to influence the currency composition of its existing long-term external liabilities in light of the country's exposure to external factors. The currency composition of the external liabilities of the country can, however, only be a useful tool in managing the exposure to commodity price movements to the extent that the movements in exchange rates and goods prices are correlated.

Hedging versus Speculative Activity

The integration of exchange risk and commodity risk management through external liability management requires decisions based on complex tradeoffs. In general, the external liability management decision can, much like the standard finance portfolio theory, be split up into a hedging and a speculative decision.[7] The hedging decision in this context should be based upon the appropriate measure of exposure of the economy to the effects of exchange rate uncertainty in relation to the behavior of relevant commodity prices and other external variables and should assume no views on future (relative) movements of exchange rates, commodity prices, and other external variables—beyond those views that the world financial markets imply through arbitrage conditions. The speculative decision involves answering the question of how the country should position the currency composition of its external liabilities in the light of its anticipations—which can be different from the market at large—regarding future developments in exchange rates, commodity prices, and other relevant external variables. The final allocation of the liability portfolio between the hedging and the speculative set should be made taking into consideration the country's risk-costs tradeoff, that is, its degree of risk aversion. This chapter, however, focuses mainly on the hedging aspect of external liability management.

The hedging component of the currency composition decision cannot be based on exchange rate movements alone, but will have to be determined in relation to the uncertainty of the *real* burden of serving the debt obligations—that is, relative to the ability of the country to generate foreign exchange. Therefore, one must take into account interactions between exchange rates and the factors that determine the ability of the country to generate net foreign exchange cash flows, such as commodity exports earnings, to service the external debt.

Relations between Exchange Rates and Commodity Prices

Changes in cross-currency exchange rates have a direct effect on goods' prices, as has been observed in the traditional inverse relationship between the dollar exchange rate and the price of (primary) commodities—at least up to the most recent depreciation of the dollar.[8] In addition, as cross-currency exchange rate changes affect the relative competitiveness of countries with which a developing country competes in a particular export market, developing countries' market shares and profit margins can be affected by movements in cross-currency exchange rates. Similar effects of exchange rate changes exist on the import side because cross-currency exchange rate changes can be expected to influence import prices. It has generally been postulated that the impact of exchange rates on intermediate goods (generally a large component of developing countries' imports) is not as strong as it is in the case of primary commodities.[9] As a result, exchanges rate changes can have a substantial impact on many developing countries because a large share of their export earnings is derived from primary and other commodities, which are exchange-rate sensitive, and because their imports (prices) can also be exchange-rate sensitive.

Hedging-Policy Guidelines

Now, some concepts and principles will be discussed that have been proposed for the hedging decision in external liability currency management, as well as the strengths and weaknesses of the proposed rules.[10] The most often proposed strategies in respect of the composition of external liabilities relate to the following: the pattern of the country's trade and other noninterest current account flows; the currency denomination of its noninterest current account export revenues or flows; and the composition of the basket of currencies with respect to the management of the domestic currency.

The pattern of trade rule implies that a country should borrow in currencies according to the distribution of its net trade (and other flows) among lender countries in the expectation that when the currency of an export market appreciates, increasing its debt service, then the borrower's terms of trade are likely to improve. This will (partially) offset the higher costs of servicing debt in that currency (and the opposite would be true for the imports of the country). The rule assumes that an appreciation of the currency of an importing country is accompanied by an increase in the exporting country's ability to pay as its exports to that market and terms of trade improve. It is not clear, a priori, that the appreciation of a currency of an export market has to mean an improvement in the country's terms of trade and an increase in debt servicing capacity. In fact, the value of U.S. imports from debtor countries dropped greatly during the time the dollar rose. Another example that demonstrates how misleading this rule is would be the situation in which two different countries were exporting the same good to the same country. The cross-exchange rate between the two exporting countries could be equally, or more, important for the relative competitiveness and market shares and market volumes of the two countries in the importing country (and, thus, for the debt servicing capacity of the countries) than the value of currency of the importing country vis-à-vis each of the individual countries.[11]

The rule to base the currency composition of external debt on the currencies of invoice or denomination of exports (or of net noninterest current account flows) could equally be criticized. There is ample evidence that the relationship between the nominal denomination and the real value of exports can, at times, be perverse. As noted before, the real price of commodities has historically been inversely related to the real value of the dollar, even though most commodities are nominally denominated and traded in terms of dollars. The inverse relationship implies that the dollar would *not* necessarily be the optimal currency in which to borrow because its value could have a perverse relationship with the country's ability to generate foreign exchange through exports of (primary) commodities—even though exports could be priced or invoiced in dollars. Because the depreciation of the dollar implies an appreciation of other currencies, a positive relationship might exist between the value of other currencies and commodity prices: When the dollar appreciates, commodity prices decline. Other currencies depreciate too, however, which might instead make nondollar currencies good external liabilities for primary commodity exporters. In sum, a currency composition based on a country's trade denomination pattern does not necessarily reduce *real* risks, and might even increase them.

The composition of the foreign currency basket with respect to which the country manages its domestic currency could itself serve as an indicator for the optimal composition of the country's external liabilities, provided the composition of the basket is determined optimally. An optimal determination of the weights in the currency basket should take into account the interaction between exchange rates and the prices of the goods the country exports and imports. It should also consider the country's relative competitiveness in export markets, the demand and supply elasticities for traded goods, the sensitivity of capital flows, and other factors that are equally important in determining the optimal currency composition of external debt.[12] It turns out that if the currency basket is indeed determined optimally in light of these tradeoffs, then its weights will be very similar to the optimal weights of currencies in the composition of external liabilities. In other words, even though the rule is largely correct, it only defers the problem to the determination of the optimal currency basket weights.

Real Risks

In general, the nominal dimension cannot be the only and necessarily correct determinant for the currency choice of external debt. If one uses the nominal denomination of trade flows, the U.S. dollar would be the predominant currency for most developing countries.[13] When it is realized that prices in world commodity and manufactures markets depend on the interaction between demanders and suppliers in different currency zones, however, it is clear that the nominal currency denomination of a good or the nominal direction of trade does not have to reflect the "real" currency denomination of the price of a commodity or manufacture. In world markets for commodities and manufactures, suppliers become more (or less) competitive depending not only on the changes in their own currency, but also on the changes in other suppliers' home currencies. Similarly, demanders will consider goods more (or less) attractive depending on the movements of the exchange rates of multiple suppliers. As a result, the changes in the price of a particular good or commodity as a result of exchange rates changes will, inter alia, depend on the type of market structure (perfectly competitive, oligopolistic, etc.). Demand and supply elasticities and, thus, the market structure play a crucial role in distributing the effects of exchange rates in terms of (nominal and real) price and quantity changes over the different market participants.[14]

The policy-oriented rules on the hedging decision discussed so far can thus be criticized as not being explicitly related to a specific goal or objective and not being based on an explicit definition and measurement of real risk. It might also be the case that these rules increase, rather than decrease, the fluctuations in the cost of borrowings over time. A more integrated approach would base the hedging decision as to the currency composition choice of external liabilities on the uncertainty of the real effective costs in a particular currency—where the costs are related to the ability of and the opportunity costs to the country in generating foreign exchange. In this approach, the real costs and riskiness of borrowing in a particular currency would depend not only on the nominal costs of borrowings and their uncertainty, but also on whether the appreciation or depreciation of a particular currency is associated with an increase or decrease in the ability of the country to generate foreign exchange. For the latter concept, one could use indicators such as the level of exports and the country's terms of trade.[15]

Speculative Aspects

So far, the discussion has centered on the hedging component of the external liability decision that was defined with respect to some underlying measure of real risk. The speculative decision has to be defined similarly with respect to some underlying measure of the real cost to service external debt. As a result, the speculative portfolio will, inter alia, depend on expectations regarding exchange rate and interest rate movements—potentially in relation to factors such as commodity price movements and to the country's risk tolerance. Because exchange rates (like all market-based prices) are very difficult to predict—and it is unlikely that developing countries have a comparative advantage in predicting them—in the context of an optimal borrowing strategy, it seems valid to use the presumption that the objective of the country in choosing its currency composition is not to "beat" the market. Market expectations of the movements of cross-currency exchange rates are related to the nominal interest differentials between individual currencies. It can therefore be expected that, under perfect market conditions, ex-ante deviations from uncovered interest rate parity are small, and expected borrowing costs will thus be similar in all currencies.[16] The currency composition choice will then become predominantly a hedging decision. In addition, it can be argued that the developing countries have relatively higher degrees of risk aversion, which would further reduce the influence of the speculative decision.

Some further theoretical development is necessary, predominantly for the hedging and less so for the speculative component of the currency choice, and, in the end, only empirical work can clarify the issue. In the next section, a theoretical model of a small, open economy is developed to determine its optimal currency composition in light of the joint behavior of commodity prices and exchange rates.

An Analytical Model for Commodity Risk and Exchange Rate Management

Consider a world that consists of a small, open economy (the home country) and N developed countries.[17] Let each of the N developed countries, in whose currencies external debt can be denominated, have an exchange rate $e(i)$, $i = 1, \ldots, N$, which follows the diffusion process:[18]

$$(7\text{-}1) \qquad \frac{de(i)}{e(i)} = v_{e(i)}dt + \sigma_{e(i)}dZ_{e(i)}, \qquad i = 1, \ldots, N$$

Here $e(i)$ is written in terms of the home country's currency per unit of the foreign currency (e.g., pesos per U.S. dollar), and $dZ_{e(i)}$ is a Wiener process. So $E(dZ) = 0$ and $VAR(dZ) = dt$. Thus, this differential equation says that the expected value of the depreciation of the ith exchange rate during the time period dt is $v_{e(i)}$ and its standard deviation is $\sigma_{e(i)}$. It is assumed that the exchange rate depreciations are approximately normal for small intervals dt and that the exchange rates themselves are lognormal.[19]

Suppose also that the means and standard deviations $v_{e(i)}$ and $\sigma_{e(i)}$ are allowed to depend on both time and a vector of state variables (which will be defined later). So,

$$(7\text{-}2) \qquad v_{e(i)} = v_{e(i)}(S, t) \quad \text{and} \quad \sigma_{e(i)} = \sigma_{e(i)}(S, t)$$

where S is a $(S \times 1)$ vector of state variables that are assumed to follow Itô processes. Thus, there are N foreign currencies in which the home country can denominate its liabilities and invest its wealth, which are assumed to follow the process

$$(7\text{-}3) \qquad \frac{de(i)}{e(i)} = v_{e(i)}(S, t)dt + \sigma_{e(i)}(S, t)dZ_{e(i)}$$

Suppose that each country in the "world" has one nominal riskless (instantaneous) bond. Let $B^*(j)$ be the price in the jth currency of the foreign country j's riskless bond and B be the price in the home currency of the home country's riskless bond. The dynamics for $B^*(j)$ are given by

$$(7\text{-}4) \qquad \frac{dB^*(j)}{B^*(j)} = R^*(j)dt, \qquad j = 1, \ldots, N$$

where $R^*(j)$ is the instantaneous nominal rate of return on the jth bond in currency j, which is assumed to be constant. Also, let R be the instantaneous nominal return on the safe domestic bond. All interest rates are assumed to be constant.

Define the excess return of the jth foreign bond for a domestic investor, $dH(B^*(j))/H(B^*(j))$, as the return on one unit of domestic currency invested in the foreign bond, financed by borrowing at the interest rate R in the domestic country, that is,

$$(7\text{-}5)\qquad \frac{dH(B^*(j))}{H(B^*(j))} = R^*(j)dt + \frac{de(j)}{e(j)} - Rdt, \qquad j = 1, \ldots, N$$

$$= (R^*(j) + v_{e(j)} - R)dt + \sigma_{e(j)}dZ_{e(j)}$$

Notice that the foreign bonds are risk-free in their own country, but exchange rate risks make them risky for investors from the "home country" and that their excess returns are perfectly correlated with the changes in the corresponding exchange rate.[20]

Next, suppose there are K commodities consumed in the home country, whose domestic currency prices follow the differential equation

$$(7\text{-}6)\qquad \frac{dP(i)}{P(i)} = v_{P(i)}dt + \sigma_{P(i)}dZ_{P(i)}, \qquad i = 1, \ldots, K$$

Again, $v_{P(i)}$ and $\sigma_{P(i)}$ are allowed to be functions of both time and a vector of state variables. So the commodity price changes have a mean of $v_{P(i)}(S, t)$ and a standard deviation of $\sigma_{P(i)}(S, t)$ over short time intervals dt.[21]

The first K elements in the $(S \times 1)$ vector of state variables are assumed to be the changes in the logarithms of the commodity prices; the next N elements are assumed to be the changes in the logarithms of the exchange rates, and the remaining $(S - K - N)$ elements are assumed to be other unspecified exogenous variables.

Finally, it is assumed that the domestic investor maximizes a time-additive von Neumann-Morgenstern lifetime expected utility function that depends only on the consumption of the K commodities and time, that is, $E_t\{\int_t^\infty U[c_1(z), \ldots, c_k(z)]e^{-\delta z}\, dz\}$ where δ is the intertemporal rate of time preference and c_i is the consumption rate of good i. This assumption completes the model, and allows one to solve for the optimal liability portfolio.[22]

Let $\mathbf{b}$ be the optimal amounts of foreign liabilities; let $\mathbf{V}$ be the $(N \times 1)$ vector of excess returns; let $\mathbf{V}_{aa}$ be the $(N \times N)$ covariance matrix of excess returns to the foreign bonds; and let $\mathbf{V}_{as}$ be the $(N \times S)$ matrix of covariances between the excess returns and changes in the state variables, which include the K commodity prices. Notice that, because the excess returns on foreign liabilities are perfectly correlated with changes in the exchange rate, $\mathbf{V}_{aa}$ is the same as the covariance matrix of exchange rate depreciations, and $\mathbf{V}_{as}$ is the same as the matrix of covariances between the exchange rate depreciations and changes in the states variables—where the first K state variables are the commodity prices.[23] It can be shown (see Svensson, 1987; Stulz, 1981; or Breeden, 1979) that the optimal holdings of foreign bonds $b = 1/C_w[-U_c/U_{cc}\mathbf{V}_{aa}^{-1}\mathbf{v} - \mathbf{V}_{aa}^{-1}\mathbf{V}_{as}C_s]$, where $C = C(W, S, t)$ is the consumption expenditure function of the investor, W is wealth, and subscripts refer to partial derivatives. Notice that this is a linear combination of $(s + 1)$ column vectors, each of which (when appropriately scaled) can be interpreted as a mutual fund portfolio. The first portfolio is a mean-variance efficient portfolio (i.e., a speculative portfolio), given by $V_{aa}^{-1}v$, and the remaining s portfolios are hedging portfolios, given by the s columns of

$$(7\text{-}7) \qquad\qquad\qquad V_{aa}^{-1}V_{as}$$

The weights in the linear combination depend on the parameters of the utility function (such as degree of risk aversion and the consumption shares of the different goods), although the portfolios themselves do not. The weight on the speculative portfolio is $-1/C_w(U_c/U_{cc})$ where U_c/U_{cc} is the inverse of the coefficient of absolute risk aversion, and the weights on the hedging portfolios are $-C_s/C_w$. For a country with a high degree of (relative) risk aversion, the hedging mutual funds will clearly be relatively more important in the overall optimal holding of foreign bonds than the speculative mutual fund. Assuming that most developing countries are relatively risk averse, and using the assumption that the expected costs of borrowings in different currencies, after adjusting for exchange rate changes, are all equal (i.e., $v = 0$), the focus of the rest of this chapter will be on hedging portfolios.[24]

The hedging portfolios are the portfolios that provide the maximum correlation with the state variables S; hence, they can be used to hedge against unanticipated changes in the state variables. This is because, after a shock to a state variable, the hedging portfolio leaves the investor's wealth and welfare "as near as possible" to what it was originally, where "nearness" depends on the degree of correlation of that portfolio with the state variable.

The state variables that are of most concern here, and against which a commodity exporting developing country would want to hedge most, are the K commodity prices that determine its welfare level. The model says that the optimal way to hedge the K commodity prices (and, thus, the consumer's welfare) against changes in the exchange rates is to borrow according to the first K elements of the matrix $V_{aa}^{-1}V_{as}$ because then a change in each currency leaves the investor's net welfare the least affected and would insulate the country from relative prices shocks, which are assumed to be the only external shocks affecting the country.[25] The hedging portfolio has to be determined in light of the interaction between exchange rates and relative (commodity) prices movements.

In the empirical application of this model, the K commodities prices have been collapsed to one price—the difference between the logarithm of the export price and the logarithm of the import price, that is, the country's terms of trade.[26] The terms of trade indicate the opportunity costs of foreign good consumption in terms of foreign goods earnings. The hedging portfolio of foreign liabilities will then insulate the country as well as possible against increases in the prices of import goods relative to the prices of export goods.[27]

Empirical Applications in Indonesia and Turkey

The Econometric Model

On the basis of the theoretical model, a portfolio of foreign assets is desired that has maximum correlation with the changes in the terms of trade.[28] This optimal hedging portfolio can be found by solving equation 7-7, where V_{as} is now the vector of covariances between the changes in the terms of trade and the changes in the exchange rates. Notice that $V_{aa}^{-1}V_{as}$ is a simple ordinary least squares (OLS) regression (without intercept) of the changes in the state variable on changes in the exchange rates. So one could calculate the optimal portfolio shares by running a simple OLS regression of the terms of trade changes on the exchange rate changes and use the parameter estimates for the slopes as the shares. This procedure implicitly assumes that the variances and covariances of the exchange rate changes are constant through time, however, an assumption that has been proven false many times in the literature. It would seem appropriate, then, to use an estimation procedure that allows the covariance matrix to change with time.

Autoregressive Conditional Heteroskedasticity (ARCH) is an econometric technique developed by Engle (1982) to do just that. In the univariate version that he presents, the conditional variance of a time series is allowed to depend on lagged squared residuals in an autoregressive manner. This means that during periods in which there are large unexpected shocks to the variable, its estimated variance will increase, and, during periods of relative stability, its estimated variance will decrease.

Kraft and Engle (1982), Bollerslev (1986), and others have generalized the ARCH model in much the same way that an Autoregressive model is generalized to an Autoregressive Moving Average (ARMA) model. This model, called Generalized ARCH or GARCH, is the same as an ARMA model in squared residuals. Just as the ARMA model allows the mean to change with time, the ARCH (and GARCH) model allows the variance to change with time. The generalization of the univariate ARCH models to multivariate ARCH models involves allowing the whole covariance matrix to change with time, instead of allowing just the variance to change with time. The model used in the application reported here was developed by Bollerslev (1987). Although somewhat restrictive (because it imposes the restriction that the correlation matrix is constant through time, while the covariance matrix changes), it is relatively simple to estimate.

The Optimal Portfolios

The GARCH process was estimated for weekly exchange rates for the five major lending currencies: Japanese yen (¥), deutsche mark (DM), Swiss franc (SwF), pound sterling (£), French franc (Ff) and U.S. dollar (US$) for nine different subperiods; each consecutive subperiod covered an additional quarter of observations.[29] Each of the nine subperiods covered the period from the first available data point until the start of the quarter for which the optimal portfolio was to be calculated. As a result, a series of (conditional) forecasts of the variance-covariance matrix of exchange rate depreciations for the next three months resulted, that is, (V_{aa}). The inverse (V_{aa}^{-1}) was calculated and multiplied by the vector of forecasted covariances between exchange rate depreciations and changes in the terms of trade, $(V_{aa}^{-1}V_{as})$.[30]

The results for the optimal portfolio shares for Indonesia are shown in table 7-1, where the portfolios are scaled to sum to one and where a negative portfolio share implies that a country should invest its foreign currency assets in the currency to hedge terms of trade risk. As can be observed, the relative shares of the currencies change quite a bit from quarter to quarter, and, as it turns out, the unscaled portfolios also change. Note, however, that the effective currency distribution of the portfolio does not change much through time once one accounts for the high correlation between the period-to-period changes of the European currencies over this period. The sums of the shares of the European currencies (DM, SwF, £, and Ff) are for each quarter (from the first quarter of 1986 through the first quarter of 1988): 10.9, 13.8, 7.4, 18, 34.4, 19.7, 25.8, 11.1, and 6.1 percent. The combined European share is

Table 7-1 *Optimal Portfolios for Indonesia*

Period	¥	DM	SwF	£	Ff	US$
1986.1	−0.005	0.307	−0.055	0.007	−0.154	0.900
1986.2	−0.022	0.320	−0.028	0.028	−0.182	0.884
1986.3	−0.001	0.164	−0.012	0.021	−0.100	0.928
1986.4	−0.027	0.384	0.019	0.027	−0.252	0.849
1987.1	−0.009	0.801	0.026	0.150	−0.632	0.665
1987.2	0.006	0.462	0.015	0.075	−0.354	0.797
1987.3	−0.033	0.703	−0.017	0.050	−0.479	0.777
1987.4	0.044	0.323	0.001	0.029	−0.243	0.847
1988.1	0.031	0.191	−0.005	0.014	−0.139	0.907

Table 7-2 *Optimal Portfolios for Turkey*

Period	¥	DM	SwF	£	Ff	US$
1986.1	0.911	−0.311	−0.893	0.255	1.131	−0.093
1986.2	0.335	−0.677	−0.589	0.531	1.265	0.135
1986.3	0.799	−0.479	−0.833	0.718	1.019	−0.225
1986.4	0.548	−0.365	−0.974	0.932	0.867	−0.007
1987.1	0.390	−0.363	−1.022	0.857	1.086	0.052
1987.2	0.362	−0.159	−0.863	0.618	1.190	−0.147
1987.3	0.237	−0.123	−1.234	0.483	1.783	−0.146
1988.1	0.115	−0.086	−1.842	0.498	2.511	−0.197

thus significantly more stable than the individual shares, a reflection of the high correlation among the European currencies.[31] The sum of the unscaled portfolio weights ranges between about 7 and 48, which suggests different absolute levels of borrowing.

Similar analysis can be conducted to find the currency portfolios that hedge against changes in export prices, export values, import prices, or import values.

Comparing these portfolios of terms of trade hedges with Indonesia's actual portfolio composition during this period suggests that a move toward the optimal portfolios could have resulted in a large reduction in the variance of Indonesia's net position, as the optimal portfolios differed substantially from their actual portfolios.[32] It turns out that rolling forward optimal portfolios (calculating each portfolio using data to that point in time) for each quarter between early 1986 and early 1988 was effective in reducing the variance of the debt service relative to the country's terms of trade, when compared with rolling forward a portfolio that had the actual currency composition of Indonesia's debt at the end of 1985. Presumably, the movement in Indonesia's borrowing portfolio away from ¥ to US$ resulted in increased stability of the country's debt service burden relative to the purchasing power of exports.

The case for Turkey was analyzed similarly. Applying the strategy described above, table 7-2 presents the optimal portfolios for each quarter. Here, one notices the large changes in the optimal portfolio shares through time, unlike Indonesia where they were relatively stable.

The sum of the unscaled portfolio weights ranged between about 0.9 and 2, suggesting, similar to the results for Indonesia, different absolute levels of borrowing. The sums of the shares of European currencies for the nine quarters were as follows: 18.2, 53, 42.6, 45.9, 55.8, 78.5, 90.9, 77.7, and 108 percent. The sums suggest a somewhat more stable weight

Table 7-3 *Optimal Portfolios, Shares Positive, for Turkey*

Period	¥	DM	SwF	£	Ff	US$	Sum
1986.2	0.075	0.000	0.000	0.337	0.349	0.239	0.554
1986.3	0.338	0.000	0.000	0.462	0.200	0.000	0.576
1986.4	0.117	0.000	0.000	0.677	0.067	0.138	0.705
1987.1	0.000	0.000	0.000	0.582	0.233	0.180	0.746
1987.2	0.020	0.000	0.000	0.436	0.544	0.000	0.759
1987.3	0.000	0.000	0.000	0.228	0.769	0.003	0.627
1987.4	0.037	0.000	0.000	0.251	0.712	0.000	0.663
1988.1	0.000	0.000	0.000	0.124	0.876	0.000	0.375

for the European currencies as a whole compared with the individual European currency weights.

There is a relatively large difference between Turkey's actual debt portfolio (as of late 1988) and the calculated optimal debt portfolios, which suggests that there was room for considerable hedging by modifying the external debt portfolio. Application of a similar methodology, as was used for Indonesia, resulted in no significant variance reduction, however, most likely because of the large volatility in portfolio shares from period to period.

Restricting the portfolio shares to be positive, that is, not allowing any investing in foreign currencies, resulted for the nine quarters in the portfolios for Turkey shown in table 7-3. Restricting the weights of the currencies to be positive led to less skewed and somewhat more stable portfolios. In addition, the sum of the unscaled portfolio amounts (the right-hand column of the table) was more stable.

Overall, the results for Turkey need to be interpreted with extreme caution because the weights turn out to be very unstable over time. This can most likely be explained by the fact that Turkey's economy has undergone significant structural changes in its export and import patterns during this period.[33] As the structure of the underlying model is changing over time, it prevents the calculation of portfolios that can serve as effective hedges. Imposing more restrictions, while solving for the portfolio weights, and/or using different econometric techniques would therefore be unlikely to lead to more stable results.

The results for both countries point up some general pitfalls in the empirics. One rests in the data for the terms of trade, which traditionally have been of poor quality for many developing countries. The major pitfall of the empirical applications, however, is most likely that the relationships between the terms of trade and exchange rates changes are not stable or sufficiently robust over time that the optimal portfolio for the next period can be determined with accuracy. Correlations between terms of trade and foreign exchange rates for both countries were relatively low. As for topics for further empirical research, several come to mind. One is to perform these types of analyses with a larger set of currencies. Another research topic would be to experiment with the use of an instrumental variable to forecast the developing country's currency changes and obtain the deviations from the expected exchange rate changes. This econometric technique might be necessary because many of the developing countries' exchange rates are not "market" rates and often do not follow the assumed random walk (in first differences). Other research extensions would be to account for the movements of the lender's interest rates in calculating the effective costs of foreign borrowings and to expand the set of possible liability instruments by including, for example, commodity-linked bonds.

Conclusion

This chapter has examined the issues involved in integrating commodity and exchange risk management. It has pointed to weaknesses in the currently accepted guidelines regarding derivation of the optimal currency composition of a country's external liability and has presented a model that can be used to calculate the optimal debt portfolio for a country that wishes to hedge against exchange rate and commodity price fluctuations. The chapter has also summarized estimates of the optimal currency composition of Indonesia's and Turkey's external debt, derived on the basis of this model. The optimal portfolio calculated for Indonesia for a recent period was an effective hedge, reducing the variance of the costs of borrowing relative to Indonesia's terms of trade. The applications of the theoretical model show that even though developing countries might have only limited access to organized currency futures and commodity hedging markets, they can manage their external exposure effectively if they can at least structure their external debt in light of the relationships between exchange rates and commodity prices.

It seems fair to conclude that there can be significant benefits from integrating currency risk management with commodity risk management, particularly as dollar/nondollar currency movements are likely to have offsetting effects on the relative level of the country's debt burden in the form of primary commodity price movements. Because many developing countries depend heavily on exports earnings from primary commodities to service their external debt obligations, a certain amount of nondollar external debt obligations could be a good external liability policy. The optimal amount of nondollar obligations and the division among the specific nondollar currencies will depend on the relationships between the commodity prices and exchange rates in question. Because these relationships might not be very strong and may be unstable over time, care has to be taken in implementing the portfolio compositions resulting from the empirical work. The policy guidelines discussed earlier might still be of use in verifying the properties of the portfolio compositions.

Notes

1. Dornbusch (1985), p. 335.
2. The World Bank, *Annual Report, 1987,* p. 49.
3. The share of dollar-denominated external liabilities of all developing countries reporting to the World Bank Debt Reporting System (DRS) hovered around 63 percent in the early 1980s and then steadily declined from 66 percent to around 50 percent in 1987. The decline since 1985 has been in part due to the depreciation of the U.S. dollar and in part due to the relative retreat of U.S.-dollar-based lenders from sovereign lending.
4. For example, the U.S.-dollar-measured level of external debt of all DRS-reporting developing countries was US$102.7 billion.
5. In general, movements in import as well as export prices have affected the developing countries. Webb and Zia (1988) have performed some counterfactual scenarios in which they demonstrate that, assuming that the change in resource flows as a result of terms-of-trade changes was met by increased or decreased external debt buildup (using the actual volumes of exports and imports in the 1980s), for a number of developing countries, their external debt in 1986 would have been substantially less (as much as 25 percent of their gross domestic product) if the terms of trade for these countries had remained at their average level of the 1969–78 period.
6. For example, well-diversified financial institutions can transform an external liability denominated in one currency into a liability of another currency through a forward transaction at a cost that can be substantially below the opportunity costs for a liability holder such as a developing country.
7. The conditions necessary to separate the hedging and speculative decision are well documented. See, for example, Breeden (1979).
8. The recent increase in commodity prices seems to confirm the inverse relationship between the dollar exchange rate and commodity prices. The slump in commodity prices in the first years after the recent dollar depreciation can be, in part, explained by developing countries' needs to raise foreign exchange through the export of commodities whose demand was inelastic. Gilbert (1988) concluded that the long-run elasticity of commodity price indices with respect to change in the value of the dollar—corrected for, among others, developing country debt servicing—was approximately unity. This would imply that commodity prices rise and fall inversely to dollar appreciation or depreciation and could have important implications for external liability management of a (primary) commodity exporting nation. He also concluded that there are suggestions that the interaction between dollar appreciation and the dollar-denominated debts has been responsible to a significant extent for the low primary commodity prices in the years during and immediately after the dollar appreciation. Dornbusch (1985) found an elasticity of the real commodity price on the real U.S. dollar exchange rate of approximately −0.82. Using lagged values for the real exchange rate, the elasticity became −1.5.

9. See Giovannini (1985) and Dornbusch (1987) for their ideas and empirical work in this regard.

10. Lessard and Williamson (1985) is a good example of this literature.

11. Of course, whether or not purchasing power parity (PPP) holds plays an important factor in this matter. If PPP held perfectly, currency fluctuations would presumably not affect real export earnings and costs of imports. For strong and conclusive rejections of PPP, see Frankel (1981) and Cumby and Obstfeld (1984).

12. For further information on the optimal currency basket literature, see Branson and Katseli (1982) and Lipschitz and Sundararajan (1982). Williamson (1982) surveyed many of the issues on currency baskets.

13. Pagee (1981) reported that, in the late 1970s, approximately 55 percent of world exports were denominated in U.S. dollars.

14. For further analysis of this issue, see, for example, Dornbusch (1987), Giovannini (1985), Flood (1986), and Varangis and Duncan (1990). Dornbusch (1987) has a simple model in which the real dollar exchange rate enters in the commodity pricing function.

15. See Ahamed (1988) for a very useful discussion on optimal currency management, which is similar to the discussion here. Ahamed mentions real income as a potential underlying variable to hedge. A rule of thumb on currency management for countries with oil exports, for example, which has been popular during some periods, was that these countries should borrow British pounds or Norwegian kroner because these currencies were more likely to be correlated with the price (and export earnings) of oil.

16. *Ex-ante* deviations from uncovered risk parity will be due, apart from transaction costs, to risk premia. As these risk premia will be largely determined in the developed capital markets that, compared with developing countries, have an advantage in carrying risk—because of factors like the wider portfolio choice in developed countries—it seems valid to argue that these risk premia will be relatively small compared with the risk-reducing benefits for the developing country involved. As long as the developing countries are more risk adverse than what the developed countries' capital markets imply, transferring risks from the developing to the developed countries can be a Pareto improvement.

17. This section is a brief summary of a restricted version of the model presented in Claessens (1988), which is also reported in Kroner and Claessens (1989). See the first paper for the general model and some further references. See Wells (1989) for similar work.

18. It is assumed that forward and futures markets for foreign exchange and commodity prices are insufficiently available to allow the country to hedge these risks.

19. See Merton (1971) and Fischer (1975) for descriptions of the properties of Wiener processes and stochastic differential equations. The general equilibrium implications of these and other assumptions are not discussed here.

20. If one had assumed that foreign interest rates were not constant, the domestic currency return on a foreign bond would not necessarily have been perfectly correlated with the exchange rate, as foreign interest movements could have offset or increased exchange rate movements. Short-term foreign currency deposits would still have a relative exposure (i.e., elasticity) of one with respect to exchange rates, but the exposure on the returns (or costs) of long-term fixed and/or floating instruments could have been different from one. Adler and Simon (1986), however, have shown that during the period from 1973 to 1980, the exposure on returns on foreign long-term bonds was essentially one with respect to their own currency and that exposure with respect to other currencies was essentially zero. This would imply that longer-term foreign liabilities would present equal hedging potential against their own exchange rate changes as the short-term instruments used here. The verdict on the post-1986 period is still out and could very well be different because the interaction between interest rate changes and exchange rate changes has, if anything, become more complex.

21. One must not assume that the law of one price holds necessarily for all goods (nor that PPP holds); that is, $P(i) \neq P^* (i, j)e(j)$ necessarily for all i and j, where $P^*(i, j)$ is the price of the traded good i in terms of foreign currency j. Neither is it assumed that changes in the terms of trade are perfectly correlated with the (weighted average of the) changes in the exchange rates.

22. The representative consumer technique is used here to mimic the situation in which the government acts perfectly in the interest of the individual citizen of the country and has instruments at its disposal to allocate (nondistortionary) transfers to private citizens. Alternatively, the government can decide to hedge only the exposure of its own welfare or revenue and expenditures streams. Depending on, among other things, whether private citizens have access to foreign financial hedging instruments, the two approaches can lead to different outcomes.

23. If the interest rates on the foreign liabilities would not have been constant, then the excess return variance-covariance matrix could not have been replaced with the exchange rate covariance matrix nor the covariance of excess returns with prices with the covariance matrix of exchange rates with prices.

24. High risk aversion in developing countries and low risk premia ($v \approx 0$) are compatible, provided the risk premium is largely determined in the lending countries and the level of risk is relatively low in lending countries.

25. The borrowing shares would apply to the country's net foreign liabilities, that is, the gross debt minus foreign exchange reserves and foreign exchange assets. The K prices should be interpreted as the prices of goods that are imported, relative to their opportunity costs in terms of domestic consumption foregone (as exports have to be generated to pay for imports). In other words, the K commodity prices are the relative terms of trade of the individual K goods, that is, individual import prices relative to the general level of export prices. Because the model does not deal with nontradable goods, it is not necessary to reflect in the relative price of goods the relative price of nontradables as well.

26. The use of one price variable—terms of trade—instead of K can be justified if the utility function to be maximized exhibits constant consumption shares. The covariances of the terms of trade with the exchange rates can then be written as a function of the covariances of the individual prices with the exchange rates. The empirical application later does not consider the use of foreign liabilities to hedge against domestic state variables or against nontradable assets. The only state variable is the terms of trade.

27. Empirical research on capital mobility has found that the extent of portfolio diversification, at least among developed countries, is too low to be explained by standard models of financially linked economies. Or, said differently, international asset markets are not used extensively to facilitate the transfer of external risks. This has led a number of researchers (e.g., Cole and Obstfeld, 1988) to conjecture that real markets, such as international commodity trade, can make international asset trade redundant, as fluctuations in international terms of trade may play an important role in automatically pooling national economic risks. As strong restrictions on preferences and technologies are required to make international asset markets completely redundant (e.g., commodity market demands have to be unit elastic with respect to price), the analyses would indicate that international asset trade (e.g., external trade) can lead to welfare-increasing risk pooling among nations—as a supplement and in addition to commodity trade.

28. This section summarizes work reported in more detail in Kroner and Claessens (1988).

29. The period covered was April 1, 1977 to March 31, 1988. The analysis itself was based on the logarithms of the exchange rates and the logarithms of the terms of trade, multiplied by 100. This is in harmony with the literature on exchange rates and gives the additional benefit of being able to interpret differenced logs as percentage changes. Recall

that the theoretical framework requires all the data to be differenced, so that one will deal with percentage changes. The five currencies chosen cover a currency share of approximately 80 percent of all developing countries' external debt.

30. The forecasts of the covariances between the exchange rate depreciations and the changes in the terms of trade turned out to be the unconditional covariances estimated over the respective period because the hypothesis that the covariances were not changing over time could not be rejected.

31. The (simple) correlation coefficients among the Ff, SwF, and DM varied between 0.85 and 0.91 during 1981–88. The correlation between the £ and other European currencies was somewhat weaker and varied around 0.63.

32. The actual portfolio composition of Indonesia's external debt for these periods is not reported here; however, it was roughly one-third yen, one-third dollars, and one-third European currencies.

33. For example, the share of Turkey's total exports to the Middle East has varied between 20 and 45 percent between 1980 and 1987. Similarly, exports to and imports from Organisation for Economic Co-operation and Development (OECD) countries have undergone significant changes, not only in (relative) levels, but, more important, also in terms of composition, as Turkey has begun to produce a different and higher valued range of products.

8

Hedging with Commodity-Linked Bonds under Price Risk and Capital Constraints

Richard J. Ball and Robert J. Myers

This chapter investigates whether commodity-linked bonds can offer capital-constrained producers an effective means of raising capital and hedging against output price risk. Two issues are examined. First, the optimal levels of commodity production and bond issue are determined for a risk-averse producer who has no initial wealth, no access to futures markets, and no conventional source of investment funds. Second, the assumption of no initial wealth and no futures markets is maintained, but producers are provided with the opportunity to obtain conventional loans, as well as issue commodity-linked bonds. In this case, interest centers not only on the output and bond issue decisions, but also on conditions under which issuing bonds or taking out conventional loans will be the dominant strategy for raising capital.

These issues are studied graphically in mean-standard deviation space. In a recent paper, Meyer (1987) has shown that expected utility maximization is equivalent to ranking alternatives based on their mean and standard deviation, provided a location and scale (LS) condition is satisfied. The LS condition is shown to hold in the case of the capital-constrained commodity producer studied here. Thus, the graphical mean-standard deviation analysis is fully consistent with an expected utility model. The advantages of graphical analysis are that proofs are simplified, and results are more intuitive. Meyer and Robison (1988) recently used the LS condition in a graphical analysis of futures market hedging under output price randomness.

Hedging with Commodity-Linked Bonds When Producers Are
Capital-Constrained

Suppose a commodity producer faces a stochastic output price at the
time resource allocation decisions are made. The producer has no initial
wealth, no access to futures markets, and cannot obtain conventional
loans. This might represent the situation of a developing country that is
experiencing debt servicing problems and, therefore, has been cut off
from new loans. The only means of raising revenue for purchasing inputs
is for the producer to issue bonds linked to the price of the commodity
being produced. The bonds mature at the time output is realized and
require the producer to pay the bondholder an amount equal to the
realized spot price of the commodity at maturity. The equilibrium bond
price is determined in a competitive market and depends on the probability distribution of the future commodity price. For simplicity, it is
assumed that the bonds have no coupon payments.

In this situation, the random profit of the producer can be expressed by

$$(8\text{-}1) \qquad \tilde{\pi} = (1 + r)[wb - c(q)] + \tilde{p}(q - b)$$

where π = profit, r = the interest rate, w = the price of the bond when
issued, b = quantity of bonds issued, q = quantity of the commodity
produced, $c(q)$ = a strictly convex cost of production function, and p =
the price of the commodity when output is realized. (The tilde denotes a
random variable at the time bonds are issued and resources are allocated.)

The producer's production and bond issue decision must also satisfy
the constraints

$$(8\text{-}2) \qquad \qquad wb - c(q) \geq 0 \qquad \text{and}$$

$$(8\text{-}3) \qquad \qquad b \geq 0.$$

These constraints indicate that production costs cannot exceed the
amount of revenue raised by issuing bonds and that the producer cannot
purchase (as opposed to issue) bonds. If the amount of revenue raised by
issuing bonds exceeds production costs, then the excess is invested by
producers at a known interest rate r.

The producer is assumed to choose a bond issue and a production level
to maximize the expected value of an increasing and strictly concave von
Neumann-Morgenstern utility function defined over profits. Notice,
however, that the random profit function (8-1) is linear in a single
random variable, $\tilde{p}$. Thus, different (b, q) combinations lead to profit
distributions that have the same shape, differing only by their position
along the horizontal axis (location) and/or their tightness around the

mean (scale). This means that the producer's decision satisfies Meyer's LS condition, which can be stated formally as follows.

DEFINITION.   A decision problem satisfies the LS condition if every two cumulative distribution functions, $F_1(\pi)$ and $F_2(\pi)$, describing elements in the choice set satisfy $F_1(\pi) = F_2(\alpha + \beta\pi)$ for all π and for some α and some $\beta > 0$.

Meyer has shown that when the LS condition is satisfied, maximization of expected utility is equivalent to maximizing a preference function $V(\mu, \sigma)$ of the mean and standard deviation of profits. From the many properties of $V(\mu, \sigma)$ that are discussed in Meyer's paper, two are particularly important for this analysis. First, the slope of a risk-averse producer's indifference curves in mean-standard deviation space is always positive:

$$(8\text{-}4) \qquad S(\mu, \sigma) = -V_\sigma(\mu, \sigma)/V_\mu(\mu, \sigma) > 0.$$

Second, $V(\mu, \sigma)$ is concave, so that indifference curves in mean-standard deviation space are convex to the origin.

Before investigating the shape of the producer's opportunity set, the following important assumption is made.

ASSUMPTION 1.   Bond issuers must pay bondholders a risk premium to hold the bonds, $\bar{p}/w > (1 + r)$.

This assumption says that the expected gross return on holding bonds is greater than the gross rate of return on a riskless asset. Because commodity-linked bonds are risky financial instruments, and the certain interest rate r is available to investors, this assumption simply states that there is the usual risk/return tradeoff among assets.

Now consider the opportunity set of a capital-constrained producer in mean-standard deviation space. The mean and standard deviation of profits are

$$(8\text{-}5) \qquad \mu = (1 + r)[wb - c(q)] + \bar{p}(q - b); \qquad \text{and}$$

$$(8\text{-}6) \qquad \sigma = |q - b|\sigma_p$$

where: $\bar{p}$ = expected output price and σ_p = standard deviation of the output price. The shape of the producer's opportunity set in mean-standard deviation space is illustrated graphically in figure 8-1. The opportunity set can be derived in three steps using 8-5, 8-6, and assumption 1.

First, suppose that the quantity produced is fixed at some level, and b is set equal to this production level, $b = q$. Substituting the equality into 8-5 and 8-6 gives $\mu = (1 + r)[wq - c(q)]$ and $\sigma = 0$. This defines a point on the μ axis that is in the opportunity set. (See figure 8-1.)

Second, suppose that the quantity produced remains fixed at q and b is decreased below the point at which $b = q$. Then differentiating 8-5 and 8-6 gives

Figure 8-1 *Optimal Bond Issues under Capital Constraints*

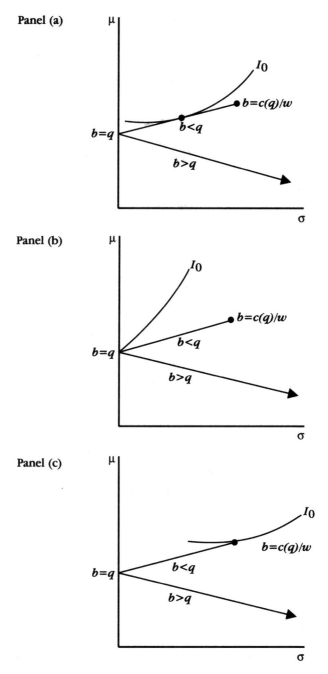

(8-7) $d\mu = [(1 + r)w - \bar{p}] \, db;$ and

(8-8) $d\sigma = -\sigma_p \, db.$

Dividing these equations gives the slope of the opportunity set as b decreases:

(8-9) $d\mu/d\sigma = [\bar{p} - (1 + r)w]/\sigma_p.$

This part of the opportunity set is indicated by the positively sloped ray moving out from the μ axis in figure 8-1. Assumption 1 ensures that the slope is positive as b decreases. Nevertheless, b cannot fall too far below q because of the capital constraint. That is, the opportunity set becomes truncated at the point at which the revenue raised by issuing bonds is just equal to the cost of producing the fixed output q. Any further reductions in b beyond this point are unfeasible because there would not be enough revenue available to purchase the inputs required to produce q. This truncation point is also illustrated in figure 8-1.

Third, suppose that the quantity produced remains fixed at q and b is increased above the point at which $b = q$. Then 8-8 becomes $d\sigma = \sigma_p dp$ and the slope of the opportunity set is now

(8-10) $d\mu/d\sigma = -[\bar{p} - (1 + r)w]/\sigma_p.$

This part of the opportunity set is indicated by the negatively sloped ray moving out from the μ axis in figure 8-1. Assumption 1 ensures that the slope of the opportunity set is negative as b increases. In this case, however, there is no truncation point because more and more revenue is being raised from bond issues.

The opportunity set shown in figure 8-1 is for changes in bond issues, while the quantity produced is kept constant. Notice, however, that changes in q simply move this opportunity set up and down the μ axis. Furthermore, because the producer prefers higher profit means to lower ones, and the slope of the opportunity set does not depend on the quantity produced, then the optimal q maximizes the intercept of the opportunity set on the μ axis. The optimal quantity produced therefore satisfies

(8-11) $c'(q) - w = 0.$

Thus, the optimal production level depends only on marginal costs and the bond price. This *separation property* is a familiar result from the literature on futures market hedging, where it has been found that the optimal quantity produced depends only on marginal costs and the futures price (Danthine, 1978; Holthausen, 1979; Meyer and Robison, 1988). Equation 8-11 shows that a similar result holds in the case of a capital-constrained producer issuing commodity-linked bonds, except that the bond price, not the futures price, is the action certainty equivalent price for the producer's output decision.

Having determined the optimal quantity produced, the next step is to characterize the optimal bond issue graphically in mean-standard deviation space. Three possible cases are illustrated in figure 8-1. In each case, the negatively sloped portion of the opportunity set is irrelevant because indifference curves are convex and positively sloped.

In panel (a) of figure 8-1, the optimum is defined by a tangency between the producer's indifference curve and the opportunity set. In this situation, the producer issues less bonds than the quantity being produced, $b < q$. The revenue raised by issuing bonds, however, is greater than the cost of production, so the excess is invested at the known interest rate r. The payout the producer expects to make on the extra bonds is greater than the sure return from investing the excess revenue. Nevertheless, the extra bonds provide an output price hedge for the producer, and this is why they are issued.

Panel (b) of figure 8-1 represents an optimum in which the slope of the producer's indifference curve is greater than the slope of the opportunity set. This is a corner solution in which the optimal bond issue equals the quantity produced, $b = q$, and the variance of profit is reduced to zero. It will occur when producers are very risk averse and want to eliminate all risk. Once again, the optimal hedge requires bond issues that raise revenue in excess of the amount required to finance production costs, and the excess is invested at the interest rate r.

Finally, panel (c) of figure 8-1 illustrates a constrained optimum in which the slope of the producer's indifference curve is less than the slope of the opportunity set. In this case, the producer is not very risk averse and would like to issue less bonds for hedging purposes (remember that the producer must pay the bondholder a risk premium to invest in the bond). Bonds sufficient to cover production costs, however, must always be issued, and so the optimum occurs at the truncation point on the upward-sloping portion of the opportunity set.

These results illustrate the effect of producer risk preferences on the optimal risk/return tradeoff from issuing commodity-linked bonds. The risk premium on the bonds causes mean profit to fall whenever the producer issues more bonds. The principal payment on the bond, however, is positively correlated with the commodity output price. Thus, the bonds provide a hedge against output price risk. If the producer is very risk averse, then there will be a complete hedge, $b = q$. If the producer is not very risk averse, then the bond issue will cover only production costs. If producer risk preferences lie between these two extremes, the revenue raised by bond issues will be greater than that required to finance production costs, but not great enough to provide a complete hedge and eliminate all risk.

Hedging with Commodity-Linked Bonds and Conventional Loans

Suppose that the producer of the previous section now has access to conventional loans at a known interest rate, r. Everything else remains as before, including the existence of a market for commodity-linked bonds. The availability of conventional loans does not change the profit function 8-1 because the producer has exactly the same revenues and costs as before. What does change is the capital constraint, 8-2. Because any amount can be borrowed or lent at the interest rate r, the producer is no longer constrained to issue enough bonds to cover production costs—the money can always be borrowed instead.

The effects that conventional loans have on optimal production and bond issue decisions are easy to derive graphically. To begin, consider the shape of the producer's opportunity set when conventional loans are available. Given some fixed level of output, q, the opportunity set for changes in b is almost identical to the previous case (without conventional loans). The only difference is that the positively sloped ray is no longer truncated at the point at which revenue from bond sales equals production costs. Because production costs can now be financed by conventional loans as well as bonds, bond issues can feasibly be reduced all the way to zero. The nonnegativity constraint, 8-3, however, continues to hold so that truncation now occurs at $b = 0$. This opportunity set is illustrated in figure 8-2.

Optimal output and bond issue decisions are characterized by consideration of preference maximization, subject to remaining in this opportunity set. Three different situations are illustrated in figure 8-2. In panel (a), the optimum is defined by a tangency between the producer's indifference curve and the opportunity set. This may occur where revenues raised from bond issues are greater than, less than, or equal to production costs. At this solution, bond sales are strictly positive and the optimal output level satisfies, 8-11. The producer is risk averse enough to hedge by issuing bonds, but not risk averse enough to eliminate all risk by setting $b = q$. Panel (b) of figure 8-2 illustrates the corner solution when the producer is very risk averse and issues sufficient bonds to reduce the profit variance to zero.

Panel (c) shows the interesting case in which conventional loans dominant commodity-linked bonds, $b = 0$. This occurs when the slope of the indifference curve is smaller than the slope of the opportunity set at the optimum:

(8-12) $$S(\mu, \sigma) < [\bar{p} - (1 + r)w]/\sigma_p.$$

Figure 8-2 *Optimal Bond Issues with Conventional Loans*

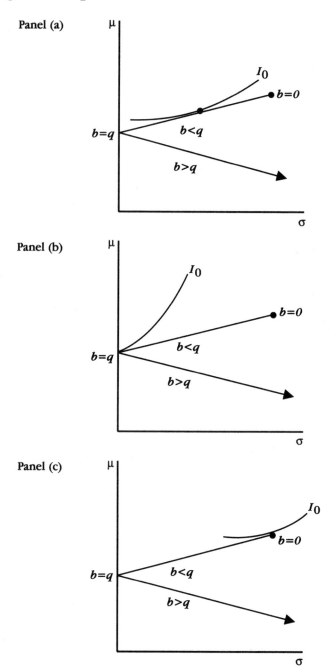

Equation 8-12 has an intuitive economic interpretation. The slope of the indifference curve represents the "cost" of producing unhedged output and bearing the full risk of output price uncertainty. The slope of the opportunity set represents the "cost" of the risk premium that producers must pay to bondholders to facilitate a transfer of risk. If this "cost" of producing unhedged output is less than the "cost" of paying the risk premium, all production costs are financed with conventional loans, and no bonds are issued. The less risk averse are producers, the more likely that conventional loans will dominate commodity-linked bonds.

The final task is to determine the optimal output level when $b = 0$. If no bonds are issued, then output is completely unhedged. Thus, at an optimum, q must satisfy

$$(8\text{-}13) \qquad S(\mu, \sigma) = [\bar{p} - (1 + r)c'(q)]/\sigma_p.$$

The slope of the producer's indifference curve in mean-standard deviation space equals the slope of an opportunity set defined by variations in q with bond issues fixed at $b = 0$.

Conclusion

This chapter examined the behavior of capital-constrained commodity producers managing output price risk with commodity-linked bonds. The study was motivated by the problems of heavily indebted developing countries that have exhausted conventional sources of credit, but still face commodity price risks. Futures markets are not available because many commodities produced by developing countries do not have futures markets, and those that do exist are typically located in major international financial centers, where developing countries may face substantial basis risk.

Results of the investigation indicate that commodity-linked bonds could have an important role to play in hedging commodity price risks. If producers are highly risk averse, and the risk premium in the bond price is "not too high," then the optimal bond issue will equal the quantity produced, and the producer will be fully hedged. As producers get less risk averse and the risk premium on the bonds gets bigger, the optimal bond issue declines. If the risk premium is high enough and producers are "not too risk averse," then no bonds will be issued provided conventional loans are available. If conventional loans are not available, only enough bonds to cover production costs will be issued.

These results were derived using a graphical mean-standard deviation approach that is fully consistent with expected utility maximization. The graphical approach is more intuitive and leads to simple proofs for the various results.

9

Financial Instruments for Consumption Smoothing by Commodity-Dependent Exporters

Brian Wright and David Newbery

Loans and other investment contracts are widely perceived as legally enforceable in lender countries but not in debtor countries. In that context, this paper shows how novel financing arrangements using commodity bonds with put options for the seller can be used to stabilize risks associated with export prices.

Given the substantial instability in all primary commodity markets, one would expect countries that depend on a single primary export for most of their foreign earnings to experience especially sharp fluctuations in export earnings and their underlying wealth.[1] To the extent that these fluctuations affect consumption, they are costly, and one would expect such countries to seek ways of managing these fluctuations, thereby reducing their costs.

In many countries, the nature of the resource endowment and its comparative advantage rule out production diversification as a significant near-term strategy, and it is not included here. In addition, diversification is ruled out via exchange of equity investments with foreigners. In this chapter, the cost of export risk is considered and commodity bonds are shown, in fact, to be capable of achieving efficient smoothing of i.i.d. export price disturbances in some cases and eventually complete smoothing in others—if that is what countries really want or need.

What are commodity bonds? Commodity bonds are bonds whose principal repayment (and perhaps dividend payments) may be made in units of physical commodity (or the terminal value of some appropriate futures contract). Typically, the bond buyer has the option to receive the nominal face value or the commodity bundle. In the finance literature, studies of the pricing of commodity bonds (Schwartz, 1982; Carr, 1987; and Priovolos, 1987a) do not distinguish bonds issued by foreign governments from private corporate bond issues. The literature on foreign borrowing, however, recognizes that the distinction is crucial.

Sovereign Borrowing and Default Prevention

The main distinction between corporate and sovereign borrowing, described in masterly fashion by Keynes (1924) and incorporated in the seminal work of Eaton and Gersovitz (1981), is that collateral is generally unavailable to creditors of a sovereign borrower because the assets of the latter are located within its borders. Only in exceptional cases can they be attached by lenders in the event of default.

The absence of a final distribution of assets to creditors, as seen in domestic bankruptcy, also changes the nature of default. It arises in the context of a sequence of strategic moves by creditors and the sovereign debtor who retains (and, in fact, cannot credibly foreswear) the power to make subsequent decisions that affect the interests of creditors.

Here, the focus is on income-smoothing financial transactions between investors in developed countries and in developing countries, which are heavily dependent on a single commodity subject to substantial revenue fluctuations. The default penalty is enforcement of debt seniority clauses in the courts of all potential borrower-lender nations, so that a defaulter's foreign investments or servicing of new debt would be subject to seizure. Default means permanent elimination of foreign borrowing or lending opportunities.

The Costs of Income Variability

Consider a country that has economically unresponsive production (zero supply elasticity) and seeks to maximize the discounted expected utility of its representative consumer

$$(9\text{-}1) \qquad V_t = E \sum_{t=0}^{\infty} (1 + \delta)^{-t} u\,(c_t)$$

where E is the expectation operator, δ is the discount rate, c_t is consumption in period t, and u is felicity, $u' > 0$, $u'' < 0$. There is no storage. Output and price are each subject to one discrete i.i.d. random disturbance per period.

To dramatize the issues, assume that exports from a single commodity account for 33 percent of GNP on average and suppose that the coefficient of variation (CV) of output and price of the commodity are both 30 percent and that the correlation between output and price can be ignored. Suppose also that all other income is nonstochastic and that the country optimally shares risks internally. There is, however, no saving or borrowing or other intertemporal income smoothing. Using the standard formulas[2] for the cost of risk, if the coefficient of relative risk aversion is R (defined for one-period variations in consumption) and if the CV of consumption is s, then the cost of risk, p, is defined implicitly by $u(\bar{c} - p) = Eu(c_t)$ (where a bar over a variable indicates its expected value), and the relative cost, $p/\bar{c}$, is approximately (exactly if utility is quadratic in income per period) $Rs^2/2$. If consumption must be equal to income each year, then $s = 0.33e$ where e is the CV of export revenue. If output and price are independently normally distributed, then $e^2 = 0.19$ (and this will hold approximately, even if output and price are not normal). In this case, if R has the not-unreasonable value of 2, the cost of risk is approximately 2 percent of average income, the amount representative consumers would be willing to forego each year in return for a stabilized consumption stream of c.

Consumption Smoothing by Borrowing and Lending

Can a country optimally smooth consumption by borrowing and lending from overseas sources? If the utility function is quadratic, then δ can be interpreted as the rate at which future consumption is discounted by the representative consumer; if this is equal to the rate of interest abroad, r, then the country has no motive for saving or borrowing other than to smooth consumption. This assumption is made here to focus on the consumption smoothing aspect of international borrowing. It is assumed that the exports are subject to random i.i.d. price disturbances. Then the optimally "smoothed" consumption of a borrower committed to borrowing and lending only for smoothing and to meeting its interest payment obligations is $c_t = E_t(c_{t+1}) = \bar{y} - rL_t$.[3] Under this scheme, accumulated debt, L, follows a discrete random walk with increment equal to the difference between income y_t and its mean, $\bar{y}$. For permanent smoothing, there must be no limit on L. In finite time, however, L will pass the value at which repudiation becomes more attractive than continued interest payments, even if all borrowing and lending opportunities are then cut off.[4] Thus, competitive lenders will not make unlimited loans. Any feasible loans would offer, at best, only incomplete and/or impermanent smoothing.

The nature of the evolution of general obligation loan contracts for sovereign borrowers is a currently active research area.[5] At this stage, it seems clear that full consumption smoothing by sovereign borrowers using conventional borrowing and lending is unfeasible if the contract is not renegotiated. If it is, then the quest for a better instrument makes sense.

Commodity Bonds Issued by Sovereign Lenders

To simplify the discussion, assume that the commodity bond under discussion is a zero-coupon bond with payment upon maturity consisting only of a completely specified commodity bundle. The issuer is assumed to be competitive and the market risk-neutral with respect to this bond. (See O'Hara [1984] for an analysis of the demand side of the market for commodity bonds under other assumptions.) As above, assume initially that all contracts are always honored.

Under these assumptions, if the country issues commodity bonds (which in this model need only be one-period bonds) and if these can be issued (and indefinitely reissued) at the present value of the expected price for next period, then their risk-reducing properties in the steady state are exactly the same as those of an optimal forward or futures hedge at the same price. Newbery and Stiglitz (1981)[6] show that, in the case of stationary, uncorrelated output and price disturbances, the ratio of income variance with and without optimal forward hedging is roughly $1/(1 + k^2)$, where k is the ratio of the CVs of price and output. In the numerical example above, k equals 1. If there is no other means of consumption smoothing by lending and borrowing, then commodity bonds will halve the steady state costs of the risk—to 1 percent of GNP in the example above. If the CV of income were the same, but only price were stochastic, then commodity bonds eliminate risk, worth 2 percent of GNP.

Assume, henceforth, that no other borrowing is possible and that all income variation is due to price. Then, with credible commitment, complete smoothing is achieved by selling commodity bonds for the whole (deterministic) output. The country then has constant income and consumption and delivers all output of random value to the lender.

In low-price states, the smoothing raises income, so there is no incentive at all to default. But in high-price states, delivery to the lender reduces current income, y_t, by $(y_t - \bar{y})$. This, plus the expected present value of autarkic future consumption, may, in some high-price states, exceed the maximum expected present value of the consumption path, given default does not occur now. Then, those states will rationally default; a no-default commitment is not credible.

The credibility of a no-default commitment by a commodity bond issuer depends on the parameters of the model. Consider the simple case with a two-point probability density for the multiplicative income disturbance that is i.i.d., $u = {}^{\pm}v$, with probabilities of outcomes $+v$ and $-v$ equal to one-half. Assume mean income is unity and utility is quadratic over the consumption range, $1 - v$ to $1 + v$. Then the annual cost of risk in the stochastic steady state (and the value of access to commodity bonds) is in this case, with all uncertainty, due to price: $\rho^* = Rv^2/2$ and the present value is $\rho^*/\delta = Rv^2/2\delta$. Now consider the stochastic steady state, in which a fraction $(1 - a)$ of output, $0 < a < 1$, is delivered each period in payment for commodity bonds issued one period earlier, and all consumption is financed from current sales of commodity bonds and the uncovered fraction (a) of output. If the income draw is high at v, then default is the expected-utility-maximizing decision if—and only if—the current period gain, $v - av$, exceeds the present value of the risk cost incurred. The change in per period risk cost is $Rv^2(1 - a^2)/2$. Default occurs if the one-shot gain exceeds the present value of the increased risk cost, that is, if $\delta \geq Rv (1 + a)/2$, so full coverage is feasible if and only if $\delta \leq Rv/2$; some fractional coverage is feasible if and only if $\delta < Rv$.

As the CV, v, the relative risk aversion, R, or the uncovered fraction a increases, the minimum δ consistent with default rises. Default on full coverage is not a problem in this case if income is risky enough and/or risk aversion is high enough.

Optimal Dynamic Smoothing Strategies

Default Constraint Nonbinding

As noted earlier, the commodity bonds may be default-free in the stochastic steady state with an i.i.d. price disturbance in which consumption equals the mean value of output, discounted one period. If so, one description of the optimal infinite horizon smoothing plan for implementation in period 0, given current income, y_0 (assumed for this exposition to be entirely from export of one commodity at price p) and the discount rate equal to the interest rate is as follows: Invest βy_0, where $\beta \equiv 1/(1 + r)$, overseas for a certain periodic rate of return of r, take out a commodity bond to cover all output, with current sale price $\beta \bar{y}$, and consume $r\beta y_0 + \beta\bar{y}$ in each period 0, 1, 2. . . . . Full efficient consumption smoothing is immediately achieved forever. (A short forward contract plus a loan on the anticipated proceeds could replicate the above contract.)

The opportunities for overseas investment at the (certain) market

COMMODITY-DEPENDENT EXPORTERS

interest rate and for sale of commodity bonds at unbiased prices are all
the financial facilities needed for this plan. Furthermore, note that if the
initial income, y_0, is invested where it can be collateralized for the
commodity bond loan (for example, in the lending country), the default
constraint is relaxed relative to the comparative static analysis above,
which assumed all income was from sales of commodity bonds and none
of the current income in the period in which commodity bonds were
introduced was saved. So, even if full commodity bond coverage seemed
infeasible in that analysis, the above strategy may work.

Default Constraint Binding

On the other hand, what if the default constraint binds? The immediate transition to full consumption smoothing is precluded. One asks what
the optimal consumption smoothing contract is in such cases, following
the analysis of Worrall (1987) and Kletzer (1988), and then sees the
extent to which it can be replicated by existing financial instruments.
Suppose the export price in any period t can take one of S values
corresponding to S states of the world, $p_t(s) = p(s) = p(1) < p(2) < \ldots$
$p(S)$, and associated with these values, the income of the country, valued
at the spot price, is $y(s) = p(s)\,\bar{q}, s = 1, 2, \ldots, S$. The optimal contingent
borrowing contract is a level of borrowing, b, and a schedule for
repayment in the next period, $M_{t,s} \equiv M(y_t - m_t, p_{t+1}(s) + 1(s))$
contingent on the price realization $p_{t+1}(s)$ that maximizes the borrower's
utility subject to the desire not to default. If the present value function is
V, then V is the solution to the problem

(9-2) $V(y_t - m_t) = \text{Max } u(y_t - m_t + b_t) + E[V(y(s) - M_{t,s})]/(1 + r)$

where y_t and m_t are the levels of income at current price p_t and debt
repayment in the current period t, and consumption $c_t = y_t + b_t - m_t$.
This is to be maximized by choosing $[b_t, M_{t,s}]$ subject to the constraint
that the borrower does not wish to default in any state s and, thus,
foregoes any future lending or borrowing opportunities:

(9-3) $V(y_s - M_{t,s}) \geq u(y(s)) + E[u(y)]/r, \quad s = 1, 2, \ldots, S$

and subject to the zero profit constraint that, for risk-neutral lenders, is

(9-4) $-b_t + \beta E[M_{t,s}] = 0.$

From the envelope condition, $u'(y_t - m_t + b_t) = V'(y_t - m_t)$, $V(\cdot)$ is
strictly concave, implying the existence of a unique optimum. The
first-order conditions from this constrained maximization problem are

(9-5) $u'(c_t) = (1 + \mu_s)V'(y(s) - M_{t,s}), \quad s = 1, 2, \ldots, S$

where μ_s is proportional to the multiplier on the default constraint in
state s, which will be zero if the constraint does not bind.

It is possible to show that, if the default constraint binds when the scheme is implemented in period t, with current repayment obligation m_t, then the optimal loan has a contingent repayment schedule that sets a floor on net income in the next period, $(y(s) - M_{t,s})$, equal to current net income, $(y_t - m_t)$, with repayment at higher income satisfying $V[y(s) - M_{t,s}] = u(y(s)) + E[u(y)]/r$. Consumption $(y(s) + b_{t+1} - M_{t,s})$ is nondecreasing in net income, $y(s)$.[7]

Assuming the default constraint precludes complete smoothing, the optimal scheme could be approximated using commodity bonds as follows: In period t, the lender issues to the borrower a loan b_t and put option to cover fixed output $\overline{q}$ with strike price P_t^* equal to

$$(9\text{-}6) \qquad P_t^* \equiv (y_t - m_t + b_t/\beta + Z_t)/\overline{q}$$

where the option premium z_t and the amount borrowed b_t solve

$$(9\text{-}7) \quad \hat{V}(y_t - m_t) = \text{Max } u(y_t - m_t + b_t)$$
$$+ E\hat{V}(y(s) - \min [y(s) - (y_t - m_t), z_t + b_t/\beta])$$

subject to the no-default constraint

$$(9\text{-}8) \quad \hat{V}(y(s) - \text{Min } [y(s) - (y_t - m_t), z_t + b_t/\beta]) \geq u[y(s)] + E[u(y)]/r,$$
$$s = 1, 2, \ldots S$$

and the zero profit condition for writer of the put, who for the purposes of this exposition is also the lender:

$$(9\text{-}9) \quad (y_t - m_t + b_t/\beta)/\overline{q} = E\{\min [p_{t+1} \cdot (y_t - m_t + b_t/\beta + Z_t)/\overline{q}]\}$$

In period $t + 1$, the maximum repayment is $m_{t+1}^* \equiv b_t/\beta + Z_t$. If the realized state s in that period is such that $p_{t+1} \leq P_t^*$, and the option is exercised by delivery of $\overline{q}$ or equivalent trades, the borrower receives the option return less repayments, $p_t^* \overline{q} - b_t/\beta - Z_t$, and the lender is paid a net sum of $m_{t+1} = y(s) - y_t$, which may be negative. Income net of repayments is the same as last year, that is, $y_{t+1} - m_{t+1} = y_t - m_t$. The smoothing arrangements of period t, $[b_t, P_t^* Z_t]$, are then replicated in period $t + 1$.

If, however, $p_{t+1} > P_t^*$, the borrower repays the lender m_{t+1}^*, sells $\overline{q}$ on the market, and retains net income $\overline{q}p_{t+1} - m_{t+1}^* = y_{t+1} - m_{t+1}^* > y_t$, then the procedure is repeated for period $t + 1$ and the new amount borrowed, b_{t+1}, is, in this case, less than b_t, but the strike price is higher to raise minimum net income to $y_{t+1} - m_{t+1}^*$).

If the default constraint is initially binding, the process evolves as follows. In the initial period (call it period 0), assuming no prior obligations, $m_0 = 0$, $y_0 = p_0\overline{q}$, consumption is raised by commodity bond sales to $y_0 + b_0$. In period 1, if the state is j, $1 \leq j \leq S$, then $y_1 = y(j) = p(j)\overline{q}$, and $m_1 = y(j) - \text{Min } [y(j) - y_0 - m_0), Z_0 + b_0/\beta]$, so that consumption is $c_1 = y_1 + b_1 - m_1 \geq c_0$. Consumption never falls; assuming the maximum price $p(S)$ has positive probability, in finite time (period w), it occurs, and $c_{w+i} < p(S)\,\bar{q}$ is constant for $i = 0, 1, 2, 3. \ldots$ (A longer maturity offers no additional advantages in this model.) In each period, an instrument that can achieve this is a zero-coupon, one-period commodity bond payable in dollars or in a specified commodity bundle at the seller's option. This instrument contrasts with the typical commodity-convertible or commodity-linked bond that contains a call option for the purchaser, rather than a put for the seller.

When the default constraint binds, this scheme is not fully efficient in general (though it is for the two-point disturbance distribution in the example above). It would be weakly dominated by the scheme presented above in which payments were fully state-contingent for each of the high states.[8] (Here the repayment m_i^* made by the borrower when the put is not exercised does not vary with the state.) Under either scheme the consumption path exhibits the same distinctive qualitative features of upward ratcheting and eventual complete smoothing of consumption, given i.i.d. disturbances. The difference in welfare effects of the two schemes in many cases will not be large, and the much greater simplicity of our commodity bonds over full state contingency gives them a strong empirical advantage.

Before closing this section, note that the theory used here assumes that sovereign defaults are penalized by withdrawal of all lending and borrowing opportunities. The historical record, however, (Lindert and Morton, 1987; Eichengreen, 1987) does not clearly show the expected differentiation in availability of loans and their terms between countries that have defaulted several times and those that have never done so. On the other hand, despite the apparently lenient treatment of sovereign defaulters, the overall *ex post* rate of return has substantially exceeded the return on lending within the creditor countries themselves. (See Lindert and Morton, 1987.) Borrowers often appear to make net repayments in circumstances in which it is difficult to demonstrate that their efforts are in their own self-interest, even where the latter is recognized as extending well beyond stabilization.[9] Resolution of these puzzles is currently an active area of theoretical and empirical investigation.

Conclusion

Consumption-smoothing could, in principle, be quite valuable to many countries in the absence of any other risk-reducing strategies. Commodity bonds can achieve consumption smoothing in the face of random export prices for commodity-dependent developing countries that dominates smoothing using other international arrangements, such as international buffer funds or attempts to create longer-term futures markets.[10] Depending on initial conditions, the smoothing may be immediately complete (and constrained Pareto optimal) and use a straight commodity bond, or it might involve a nondecreasing consumption path, which becomes constant if and when the highest income level is attained. In the latter case, the bond could be constructed as a conventional loan with attached put for the seller; equivalently, it could be constructed as a bond with a nominal face value at maturity and an attached commodity value, delivery of either to be at the seller's option. This type of commodity bond contrasts with the observed forms, which generally offer the buyer a similar choice. The consumption-smoothing achieved reduces downside exposure of the seller, while leaving the seller a sufficiently large share of high realizations so that there is no temptation to default.

Although this has only been shown in the case of pure price uncertainty with i.i.d. disturbances (and, hence, no interperiod storage), availability of a constant risk-free rate of return and market risk neutrality of lenders, the results suggest further investigation of the smoothing possibilities of these instruments in more general circumstances. Whether such smoothing is what commodity exporters want or need is another question. Continued access to the benefit of income-smoothing, however, is often identified as a major inducement for honoring loan contracts originally motivated by other objectives such as economic development (Eaton, Gersovitz, and Stiglitz, 1986), although the observed procyclical nature of much borrowing raises questions about the smoothing objective (Gersovitz, 1985). (See also, Fishlow, 1987.) Integration of this analysis with the extensive literature on swaps, renegotiations, and related matters is an obvious extension of this approach.

Notes

1. This chapter is a substantial revision of an invited paper for the 1988 Winter American Social Sciences Association Meeting for the session, "Financial Risk Management Needs of Developing Countries," which was published under the same title in the *American Journal of Agricultural Economics*, vol. 71, no. 2 (May 1988). We thank, with the usual caveat, Doug Christian for research assistance; Jim Vercammen, Ken Kletzer, and Tim Worral for pointing out errors in a previous draft; and seminar participants at the University of California-Berkeley and Larry Karp, Ken Kletzer, Peter Lindert, and Barry Eichengreen for helpful discussions.

2. If consumption c is a random variable with a coefficient of variation s, $u(E(c) - p)$ $= Eu(c)$. Expand both sides in a Taylor series: $u(E(c)) - pu'(E(c)) \approx u(E(c)) + 0.5s^2 E(c)u''(E(c))$ or $P/E(c) \approx 0.5s^2 R$.

3. Newbery and Stiglitz (1981), pp 201–02.

4. If only borrowing opportunities are lost, but the country may invest the payments it saves overseas at the same interest rate, it can actually achieve exactly the same consumption stream for periods beyond $t + k$, as if it did not default (or never borrowed at all). See Bulow and Rogoff (1988). The partial smoothing is similar to that achieved by commodity storage. See Wright and Williams (1982).

5. See Eaton, Gersovitz, and Stiglitz (1986) for a recent survey. See also Kletzer (1988) and Bulow and Rogoff (1987). Alternative instruments are reviewed in Lessard and Williamson (1985).

6. Newbery and Stiglitz (1981), p. 186.

7. Worrall (1987), pp. 5–6, Results 1–3.

8. This difference was pointed out by our colleague, Ken Kletzer; the issue was also mooted in a private communication by Tim Worrall.

9. There is a significant body of literature following the pioneering work of Feder and Just (1977) on estimation (as distinct from explanation) of debt-service behavior.

10. See Finger and de Rosa (1980) for a cautionary analysis of the Compensatory Finance Facility of the IMF. Finger and de Rosa found that, on average, it did not even stabilize the annual export incomes of participants.

10

Securitizing Development Finance: The Role of Partial Guarantees and Commodity Contingency

Ronald Anderson, Christopher Gilbert, and Andrew Powell

Throughout the 1980s, the scale of indebtedness of many developing countries has, in conjunction with high interest rates and adverse terms of trade, meant that very little new private finance has been available to them. The lack of finance for investment has been a major impediment to economic growth in these countries. At the same time, the poor service record on much of this debt has created major balance sheet problems for creditor banks.

The largest component of developing country debt in private hands is in the form of general obligation bank loans. It is widely acknowledged that these problems would be lessened if this general obligation debt could be, in whole or in part, securitized—that is, if it could be traded in more or less standard form on liquid secondary markets, in the same way as are developed country bonds. Securitization would provide market valuations of existing debt and would allow debtor countries to raise new finance on terms that reflect their repayment potential; it would also permit creditor banks to adjust their balance sheets at relatively low cost. A number of proposals aimed at securitization have been proposed during the past few years, but, to date, none has attained any marked degree of success.

The major difficulty standing in the way of securitization is that debts of developing country governments and their immediate agencies bear sovereign risk. In circumstances in which private-sector debtors fail to honor contractual obligations, it is possible for the creditors to take enforcement action through the courts. This possibility is not open to creditors when the counterpart is a sovereign government. In such cases, debt service is, in an important sense, voluntary. Sovereign risk is therefore a major source of the illiquidity of current developing country debt. A prospective purchaser of an existing obligation must make detailed enquiries into the debtor country's economic and political situation, its likely need for new finance (which will provide an incentive to service current obligations on schedule), and its other outstanding obligations. Obligations of different countries will trade on different terms even in situations in which the contractual conditions are identical. Different potential purchasers will put different valuations on the same debt depending on their differing abilities to obtain service.

The sovereign risk problem has been seen as intractable; however, progress is possible through a two-pronged attack. First, it is necessary to separate the default (sovereign) risk component of the risk associated with the debt. Then it is possible to associate this default risk with a third-party guarantee priced at an actuarially fair rate. This guaranteed debt could then either trade in the same way as obligations issued by developed country governments or could provide the collateral against which new securities would be issued. The insurance premia associated with these obligations may be so high as to make the provision of insurance appear unfeasible. The second component of the plan is to find means of reducing the likelihood of default risk and, therefore, the size of the default insurance premia as well.

To analyze the likelihood of default, a formal model of the default-rescheduling process is required. Using an extensive form game, an expression for the rescheduled payments is derived; if rescheduling takes place and the conditions under which default will be threatened are changed, then rescheduling negotiations will follow. It is this latter condition that is crucial to the argument. It combines "willingness to pay" with "ability to pay." Throughout the 1980s, general obligation debt has carried the implication that developing countries' ability to pay has been negatively associated with their contractual obligations, and this has resulted in high default probabilities. Adjustment of contractual debt repayment terms to give a positive association between ability to pay and contractual obligations will result in significantly lower default probabilities and, therefore, in lower default insurance premia.

An obvious mechanism for obtaining the required positive association is to introduce commodity price contingency into contractual debt obligations. This proposal replaces standard interest payments with a mixture of interest payments and payments linked to primary commodity prices. Powell and Gilbert (1988) argued that this form of debt would be advantageous to developing countries that have high levels of commodity price dependence. Here, the argument may be generalized because it is possible to see any country as a portfolio of productive assets, many of which will be associated with the price of an internationally traded good. Consequently, countries can issue a portfolio of debt with the associated repayment characteristics, and each of these components of the overall portfolio can provide the basis for a secure obligation.

The chapter is organized as follows. First, a model of sovereign debt is developed. Then, the general terms necessary for securitizing debt will be discussed, including a brief reference to the experience in securitizing mortgage debt. Next, the model developed initially is applied to the main problems faced in securitizing developing country obligations. Several different instrument designs are compared in an effort to determine those most suitable for securitization. Finally, the institutional framework in which these securities could be issued is examined.

Sovereign Risk

In standard financial applications, a default occurs when one of the parties to a contract fails to honor the terms of the contract. When the borrowing party is a country, the conditions that imply default are rather elastic; a default occurs whenever the lender declares that the borrower has violated the terms of the obligation. This approach emphasizes that the declaration of default is an option available to the lender that the lender may not wish to exercise.

In a private financial contract, declaration of default will trigger legal actions that will give the lender all or part of the sums owed. These actions are not available if the borrower is a sovereign nation or its immediate agent. In the case of sovereign debt, the declaration of default may penalize the borrowing country by denying it subsequent access to international credit markets. Recourse to this action may be relatively infrequent for the reason that declaration of default removes the threat of sanctions and, therefore, reduces the prospect of recovering the sums owed.

A simple framework for understanding sovereign risk is an adaptation of a model used by Eaton, Gersovitz, and Stiglitz (1986). The default decision is based on a comparison of the cost of honoring the contract terms with the penalties resulting from default. The borrowing country will choose to not honor the contract if its payments exceed the penalty.

Figure 10-1 *The Default Decision*

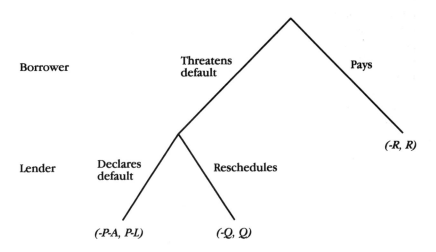

This, in turn, will lead to a rescheduling decision on the part of the lender. This can be illustrated as the simple extensive form game in figure 10-1. Here, the amounts in parentheses are the flow payoffs to the borrower and the lender respectively.

The borrowing country is scheduled to make a payment of R to the lender, but alternatively may threaten default. In that case, the lender may declare default, resulting in the borrowing country making some cash payment, P, as a penalty. In addition, the borrowing country will lose future access to capital markets. Thus, if A is the value of this access, the net payoff to the defaulting country is $-P - A$. The lender will receive an amount $P - L$ where L is the deadweight loss associated with declaring default.

On the other hand, if the lender faced with nonperformance does not declare default, the lender will enter into a negotiation to determine a payment, Q, of the rescheduled loan. The lender will choose negotiation if $Q > P - L$. What will determine Q? Because by agreeing to reschedule, the deadweight loss L and the loss of access A are avoided, it appears that there is an incentive to bargain. The rescheduling negotiation can be represented by the Nash bargaining game depicted in figure 10-2. Any successful bargain must leave each side as well-off as in formal default. The outcome most favorable to the borrowing country is at β where $Q = P - L$. The best outcome for the lender is at α where $Q = P + A$. Thus, in figure 10-2, the bargaining set is confined to the segment of the

Figure 10-2 *The Rescheduling Subgame*

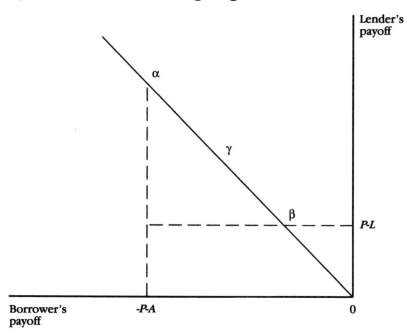

downward sloping 45 degree line to the northeast of the threat point $(-P - A, P - L)$. Any point in this set would be a conceivable solution and can be represented by

(10-1) $$Q = P + wA - (1 - w)L$$

for $0 < w < 1$. For example, setting $w = 0.5$ gives point γ and constitutes the Nash bargaining solution to this game.

This model implies that payment will be made according to schedule if $R < Q$. Using equation 10-1, one sees that this arises if $A > [R - P + (1 - w)L]/w$. That is, if for the borrowing country the value of future access to capital markets is sufficiently high, it will pay on schedule. Otherwise, it will threaten default. Taken strictly, the model implies that default will never occur because rescheduling will always offer a Paretian improvement; in practice, default threats by sovereign debtors typically do result in rescheduling.

This model may seem to overstate the case for Walter Wriston's view that "countries don't go bust." In fact, when lenders deal repeatedly with sovereign borrowers, there can be a role for formal declarations of default in that these may enhance the creditor's reputation as a tough negotiator. This bargaining power would tend to translate into an expectation of favorable future bargains for the creditor (a high w) and, thus, a high value of Q. The result would be to reduce the frequency of nonperformance. A full discussion of these reputational issues can be investigated in a repeated game extension of the model (Grossman and van Huyck, 1985).

The approach to sovereign risk adopted here stresses the voluntary nature of both debt service payments and default declaration. This does not imply, however, that contractual terms are irrelevant because, as noted here, the service obligation determines the set of circumstances in which default will be threatened and rescheduling will take place. Thus, although this approach is closer to the "willing to pay" model, "ability to pay" does play an important role. In particular, if the default penalty P and the value A of access to credit are treated as state dependent, the rescheduled payment is,

$$(10\text{-}2) \qquad Q(s) = P(s) + wA(s) - (1 - w)L.$$

In favorable states for the borrower, resulting perhaps from strong demand or high prices for its exports, the borrower is likely to perceive a high value $A(s)$ of future access and will be aware that the lender can extract a higher default penalty $P(s)$. Consequently, if scheduled payments, R, are not state dependent, the borrower is likely to pay on schedule. In adverse states, the opposite holds, and the country is likely to violate the schedule. Notice that the way in which "ability to pay" feeds into the borrower's and lender's decision process is very different to the often mechanistic relationships used in the "solvency" literature.

This general formulation is compatible with a variety of specifications of penalties that have appeared in the literature. Cooper and Sachs (1985) and Sachs and Cohen (1982) assume that the penalty to default is proportional to income, Gersovitz (1983) introduces a penalty that is dependent on the importance to the debtor of the opportunity to trade, and Eaton and Gersovitz (1981) employ a penalty dependent on the country being excluded from the market for physical capital. Each is a special case of this formulation.

Even a powerful creditor will not be able to assure performance if other factors create a strong incentive to threaten default. That is, in the terminology of the model here, even if the creditor can bargain hard (achieve a high w), the borrower may still threaten default because the payment terms (R) are severe, the default recovery (P) is low, or the value of future access (A) is low. Clearly, the nature of these variables is crucial to the predictions of this model.

The value of future access to credit markets (A) will reflect the developing country's perception of the likely future demand for its products. This, in turn, will depend on the country's resources and capabilities, the level and mix of world product demand, and the pattern of international trade barriers. There is little that can be said about these within the scope of this chapter. It is clear, however, that anything that is conducive to the prospects for future development will tend to raise A and, as a result, to reduce the problem of sovereign risk.

The creditor's loss of declaring default (L) includes the direct costs of exacting a penalty from the borrower. More important than this, however, could be the indirect effects of a declared default. Banks may maintain nonperforming loans on their books at full value. Were they to declare a default on the loans, they would be forced to take a charge against the capital of the firm. This in turn could mean that they would not meet capital adequacy requirements, thus forcing them to shrink their entire balance sheet. Creditors in this situation may place a very high value on the loss of declaring default. The model used here suggests that this tends to enhance the probability of threatened default. However, if a creditor has made an effort to remove this constraint through the provision of loan loss reserves, L need not be so large. Our model shows that this tends to improve the renegotiated terms for the creditor with the effect of decreasing the likelihood of default.

The value of the payment (P) that can be extracted upon default will depend upon the legal means available to the creditor for enforcing the contract. In the most extreme form of sovereign risk, the creditor has no legal recourse ($P = 0$). Somewhat counter-intuitively, this apparent advantage for the debtor will mean that nonperformance will be viewed as relatively more likely, so that amounts that can be borrowed at given terms will be limited. A sovereign borrower can overcome this problem by precommitting to relatively severe penalties in case of default. The most obvious way that this can be done is by placing some significant asset as collateral in an entity that falls under some legal regime other than that controlled by the borrower. It may be that a particular contract form may have a legal status that is relatively advantageous from this viewpoint. This point, as well as the possibility that payments schedules (R) can be written to minimize nonperformance, is addressed later in this chapter.

Securitization

A security is generally taken to be a financial obligation whose terms are standardized so that the holders of a particular type of security will be treated equally. Standardization is important in determining whether an instrument is traded successfully in a secondary market. When a secondary market is active, a holding in the security may be quite liquid in the sense that it could be sold quickly without a great effect on its price. Secondary trading is also promoted when a security's credit risk is readily assessed. If an issuer's credit standing is not well established, its securities may be very liquid if they have been guaranteed by a separate, credit-worthy institution.

Typically, an elaborate and costly process is involved in the issuing of securities, including registration with regulators, legal drafting, and marketing. What are the merits of securitization that justify these costs? The principal advantage of issuing securities derives from the liquidity that can result. By making it possible to trade in and out of positions in a security, the range of investors who may be willing to hold it is expanded. Consequently, the supply of funds is increased, and the price paid for the funds is reduced.

A further implication of active secondary trading is that the value of the security is established in the marketplace. By contrast, an existing bank loan that is held on the books of the originating banks is not typically valued in a market. Consequently, because of changing market conditions or the conditions of the borrower, variations in the value of that obligation are not typically reported, except in extreme cases such as nonperformance. In the terminology of principal-agent theory, the lending institution is the principal, and the borrower is the agent. The observability of actions taken by the borrower will be enhanced because market prices aggregate information available to a wide group of agents. As a result, actions that tend to decrease the value of the securities will be discouraged. In this way, market valuation of securities provides an element of discipline for managers.

Although these arguments are most often applied to private profit-making enterprises, they are equally valid in the context of sovereign borrowing. One of the major problems with the current structure of developing country debt is that it is borne most heavily by the shareholders of the commercial banks in developed countries. Providing access to other sources of finance would be a major advantage for many developing countries, and market valuation of these debts would provide reassurance to bank shareholders. Furthermore, the price of existing securities will indicate the terms that developing countries will likely face on new issues, and this provides an incentive to maximize the value of these securities.

The fact that a very large proportion of developing country borrowing has taken the form of general obligation bank loans despite the advantages of securitization is testimony to the obstacle to securitization resulting from sovereign risk. It will not be possible to completely eliminate these difficulties, but it may be possible to minimize their impact. This can be done, first, by isolating the sovereign risk from the other components of risk and, second, by adopting contract specifications that reduce the former component at the expense of the latter.

Securitizing Developing Country Obligations

In considering expanding the scope of securities in development finance, interest has tended to focus on debt/equity swaps. The use of equity finance may have considerable potential in some development projects. Its use in the presence of sovereign risk, however, is likely to be restricted. The reason is that equity is a claim on a residual profit stream. The performance of the stock will depend upon the actions of the managers of the assets. When monitoring and control are difficult, there is an agency problem, which means that the return to shareholder equity can suffer. Such problems have the potential of becoming extreme in the presence of sovereign risk. Consequently, one would expect considerable investor reluctance to acquire the residual income claims against sovereign borrowers.

Banking relationships are widely recognized as means of overcoming problems of asymmetric information. This may explain the widespread reliance on general obligation bank loans for development finance in recent years. The performance of these loans in the 1980s has made it clear that even if such relations are advantageous from the point of view of information, the problem of sovereign risk can mean that bank loans may be de facto residual income claims. Recognition of this has meant that banks have been resistant to extending further general obligation country loans.

Recent experience has shown that a number of activities that were previously thought of as the exclusive province of bank lending can be successfully given access to securities markets through appropriate instrument design. A prime example of this has been the development of the secondary mortgage market in the United States. The U.S. mortgage market is complex; however, most of the new securities used in this industry, referred to as mortgage-backed securities (MBSS), fall along fairly standard lines.[1] In most cases, the underlying assets in the security are individual mortgages that are, to some extent, standardized with respect to terms (e.g., maturity date, coupon rate, and so on). Typically, these underlying mortgages imply a certain risk that the property will default, in which case the mortgage holder receives the liquidation value of mortgaged property. Furthermore, property owners typically have the option to prepay so that the mortgage holders are uncertain with respect to the duration of these obligations.

The process of creating an MBS can be viewed as the splitting of the risks contained in a set of mortgages. First, in most cases, an MBS is endowed with a guarantee against default granted in return for an insurance premium by some third party. The MBS itself is a title to a proportionate share of the total revenues from the underlying mortgages including interest, scheduled payments of principal, prepayments of principal, and default insurance claims.[2] In effect, the insuring body assumes and prices the default risk. The prepayment (i.e., duration) risk is reduced through the effect of the law of large numbers applied to a pool of mortgages. The remaining prepayment risk and the interest rate risk are left to be priced in the market for MBSs.

The rapid development of the U.S. MBS market suggests that if it is possible to isolate and guarantee performance risk, the remaining components of risk may be assumed and priced by the market.[3] Analogously, an important step toward facilitating the securitization of developing country obligations would be to find a means of channeling the sovereign risk component of these obligations into the hands of those who have a comparative advantage in bearing this risk.[4] The vehicle for accomplishing this would be for the appropriate body to insure the performance of the developing country loans in return for an insurance premium. In the case of nonperformance by the borrower, the insurer would pay the lender the scheduled payment and, in return, would assume the nonperforming loans as a portion of its portfolio. The insurer would then negotiate rescheduling with the nonperforming borrower against the threat of declaring the borrower in default.

An important question is which agency or agencies should provide performance guarantees. Experience in the MBS market indicates that the guarantees may originate from either the private or the public sector. Thus, the Government National Mortgage Association (Ginnie Mae) is a public-sector body, the Federal National Mortgage Association (Fannie Mae) is a quoted corporation with agency status, and the Federal Home Loan Mortgage Corporation (Freddie Mac) is a private corporation also with agency status (Thygerson, 1985).

An agency will have a comparative advantage in this function if it can offer this insurance at a lower premium than other agencies. From figure 10-1 and equation 10-2, one notes that, allowing for general contingent payoffs, $R(s)$, the insurance premium will be

$$(10\text{-}3) \qquad \int_{R(s) > Q(s)} (R(s) - Q(s))f(s)\, ds$$

where $f(s)$ is the density function of states of the world.[5] It follows that an agency will have a comparative advantage in offering this insurance if it can negotiate rescheduling on terms favorable to lending institutions— that is, with high values of $Q(s)$.

There are two components to this. First, certain institutional arrangements will result in higher penalties $P(s)$ being imposed on defaulting borrowers and will be more effective in denying future access to credit markets, increasing $A(s)$. Second, different institutional arrangements will give the negotiating body greater or lesser power, thereby changing the value of w. Both considerations argue against arrangements in which the default risk is borne by a large group of individually small investors because, under those arrangements, no single investor would be able to impose significant penalties on defaulters or would have an incentive to extend a major effort in renegotiating with the developing country. Consequently, developing countries would both have favorable threat points and considerable bargaining power. In figure 10-2, the outcome of the bargaining process is likely to be nearer β than α; furthermore, β will be close to the origin.

The implication is that insurance is more likely to be available on favorable terms if the sovereign risk is assumed by a "club" of lending banks, or their agency, or by some existing or new (private- or public-sector) agency set up for this specific purpose (as in the MBS market). The fact that such an organization would be expected to deal repeatedly with developing country borrowers and develop a reputation for toughness suggests that a continuing agency dedicated to this objective is likely to perform this task better than either an informal consortium or a preexisting organization with other and potentially conflicting objectives.

Developing country loans, in combination with the insurance just described, could constitute the basis for a new security. The holders of the security would be entitled to the scheduled payments of the obligations plus any claims paid by the insurer, less a fee for the bank or other financial intermediary that services the performing obligations. Because they would be insured against credit risk, these securities would have the prospect of active secondary trading. Furthermore, the new securities could be standardized in the sense that the obligations of two developing countries could be required to conform to a standardized payoff profile. If they were, the countries would be valued the same by the market. This element of standardization would also enhance the liquidity of these securities.[6]

The Design of Commodity-Contingent Instruments and Associated Guarantees

In principle, this framework implies a simple criterion for determining those securities most appropriate for issue by developing countries. Securities with different payoff profiles, $R(s)$, will generally imply different likelihoods of default and, consequently, different insurance premia. One criterion for security design is to minimize the insurance premium, subject to the constraint that the default-risk-free value of the securities equals or exceeds the finance required.[7] Given the functions, $P(s)$ and $A(s)$, this is a straightforward problem.

In practice, the functions $P(s)$ and $A(s)$ are not necessarily well known so that the issue of optimal contract design would require considerable investigation. Here some of the considerations that appear important in light of recent experiences are noted. First, consider the general specification of a contingent instrument, $R(s)$. Note that in the 1980s, many commodity-dependent developing countries found that repayments due, $R(s)$, were high in those states precisely when incomes were low. This negative association of $Q(s)$ and $R(s)$ makes threatened default and rescheduling a very likely outcome in states adverse for the borrower. In contrast, writing contract terms so that $R(s)$ is positively correlated with $Q(s)$ would reduce the probability of default risk.

Earlier, it was suggested that $Q(s)$ is likely to be positively correlated with current and anticipated future export earnings $X(s)$. This suggests making the repayments schedule state dependent through $X(s)$ as $R(X(s))$. There are, however, two strong arguments against this proposal. First, contingency on export revenues will introduce moral hazard considerations through output and stock decisions. Second, this form of contingency would work against standardization—a contract issued against Zaire's export revenues would have different characteristics from a contract against Peru's export revenues, even though both countries are major copper exporters. Provided that markets are competitive, both difficulties can be circumvented by introducing contingency through internationally quoted prices and exchange rates.[8] If the relevant price is $C(s)$ and if the developing country's obligations are contingent on the price, $R(C(s))$, the country's scheduled net revenues in state s for one unit[9] of exports are,

$$(10\text{-}4) \qquad Y(s) = C(s) - R(C(ss)).$$

If the default penalty, P, and the value of future access, A, are functions of the price of the country's product, the condition to induce the borrower to respect the contract terms can be written as

$$(10\text{-}5) \qquad R(C(s)) < P(C(ss)) + wA(C(ss)) - (1 - w)L.$$

When the obligation is straight debt, the payment is a constant in all states, $R(s) = R_0$. If for low values of the commodity price the penalty and value of access are low, then there will be a critical commodity price C^* below which the country will have an incentive to threaten default. That is,

(10-6) $R_0 > P(C(s)) + wA(C(s)) - (1 - w)L$ for $C < C^*$.

This situation is broadly what has been demonstrated by the experience of many developing countries in the 1980s and provides the basic motivation for seeking to introduce some form of commodity contingency in the payments of the developing countries.

A basic way of introducing commodity contingency when a project faces commodity price uncertainty is to protect against low commodity prices by hedging in forward or futures markets if they are available. More specifically, by financing through a combination of straight debt and forward sales at a forward price F, the payment terms become,

(10-7) $R(C(s)) = R_0 + C(s) - F.$

This will assure a constant income $Y(s) = F - R_0$ under the contracts, although this does not necessarily assure an incentive to fulfill the contract terms. For, under 10-7, the inequality 10-5 may or may not be maintained in all states depending upon the precise way that $P(C(s))$ and $A(C(s))$ vary with C. If $P(C) = C$ and the hedgeable value exceeds the fixed payment, $F > R_0$, however, then 10-5 necessarily will hold. In fact, one of the possible advantages of a commodity forward contract at a market falling outside of the borrower's legal jurisdiction may be precisely that, in case of default, the borrower's commodity deliveries in the market may be attached through legal means.

Several considerations suggest that straight debt combined with forward sales may not be the best means of assuring that the problem of sovereign risk is reduced to the point that insurance would be feasible. One problem that arises with this combination is that it generally creates two credit risks, not one. To illustrate how this could have adverse effects, suppose that the commodity price is low. The borrower will simultaneously have an incentive to perform on the forward sale and yet to threaten default on the debt contract if the depressed commodity price reduces the value of access and if the penalty on the debt contract is low or nonexistent. One way around this is to make the forward contract itself part of the collateral for the debt contract. The alternative would be to combine the payment features of the debt plus forward sale into a single instrument—that, in effect, would become a commodity-contingent bond.

Even if combining the characteristics of straight debt and a forward sale into a commodity bond can reduce the problems of multiple credit risks, it does not necessarily assure that relation 10-5 will hold in all states. In particular, because, under 10-7, the payment rises with the commodity price, favorable states might create an incentive to default if P and A do not rise to keep pace with the commodity price. It may well be that if a commodity producer can retain the profits of a commodity price boom, the value of future access to credit may not rise and may actually fall as C rises beyond a certain range. A package to circumvent this problem is a combination of straight debt, the sale of a commodity forward at F, and the purchase of a commodity call with a strike price $K > F$, which can be written as,

(10-8) $R(s) = R_0 + C(s) - F - \max(0, C(s) - K)$

Thus, the maximum payment would be $R_0 + (K - F)$.

So far, this discussion has ignored a number of constraints that may impinge on instrument design. For instance, the schedule outlined in equation 10-8 may imply zero or negative payments in some states if commodity prices fall below a critical level (i.e., if $C(s) < F - R_0$). This feature may be unacceptable to investors. A solution to this would be to design an instrument that possessed both a minimum and a maximum payoff. For example, straight debt combined with a call purchase and written call at a lower strike price results in

(10-9) $R(s) = R_0 + \max(0, C(s) - K_1) - \max(0, C(s) - K_2)$,

where $K_2 > K_1$. This double-call feature guarantees a minimum payment $R(s) = R_0$, it has a range of commodity prices in which payments increase as the commodity price rises, and it has a maximum payment of $R(s) = R_0 + K_2 - K_1$. If penalties from nonpayment fall when commodity prices fall below K_1, this type of instrument will necessarily increase the insurance premium. This feature might be viewed as necessary to ensure that a sufficient volume of funds is forthcoming from investors.

In this discussion, the institutional structure that would be most effective in the process of securitization has not been specified. In fact, many arrangements might be effective. An interesting possibility is to consider the guarantee as a put option on the value of the loan. Thus, the holder of the guarantee pays a premium and obtains a put option covering a portion of the loan at a specified exercise price. The holder of the put compares the value of that portion of the loan covered with the exercise price of the option and exercises the put if the value of the loan, for whatever reason, falls below the exercise price. On exercising the put, the holder receives the exercise price, and the put writer assumes that portion of the loan covered. Note that, if the writer of the put has a comparative advantage in bearing sovereign risk, then there should be a

Figure 10-3 *A Financing Structure*

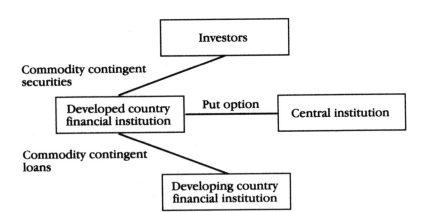

premium for the put that would be acceptable to the purchaser, but that would make put writing on average profitable.

The flexibility of this arrangement is very great indeed. In particular, the maturity of the put option and the times within its life that it may be exercised (referred to as "exercise windows") can both be altered. Furthermore, the exercise price of the option can be fixed at particular levels and could, in principle, be made contingent on the commodity price. This flexibility can be used to design a guarantee that provides maximum insurance against sovereign risk elements at minimum cost.

Figure 10-3 illustrates the concept of the put option guarantee for a given set of relations between various institutions. The developed country financial institution could be a commercial bank with existing loans to a particular developing country or might be a new type of lender entirely. The characteristic of this structure is that the lender offers commodity-contingent loans and issues commodity-backed securities to a wide class of investors. Attached to the commodity-contingent loans are put options held by the developed country financial institution covering some portion of the loan to the developing country. These options will ensure a higher credit rating for securities backed by such loans. The put option guarantee separates out significant elements of the sovereign risk from other types of risks—akin to the separation of different types of risks in the U.S. mortgage backed securities market discussed earlier.

These instrument designs and potential lending structures are only intended to be illustrative of the implications of this discussion of sovereign risk. Considerable further research is required. Given more precise information on the nature of default penalties and the value of access and investor preferences, it should be possible to design appropriate payment schedules and structure guarantees to suit.

Conclusion

It has been argued here that insured, contingent-payoff securities could replace much of the general-obligation governmental borrowing as a source of developing country finance. Furthermore, for reasons of standardization and moral hazard, income (export revenue) contingency is a less promising avenue than contingency on a publicly observable, nonmanipulatable variable such as competitive commodity prices or exchange rates. A possible objection to this is that contingency on commodity prices and foreign exchange may be of limited relevance to many larger and more diversified developing countries, particularly those with substantial exports of manufactures. These problems are not insurmountable. A country may be viewed as a portfolio of productive assets, each having a value more or less linked to the price of its good(s) in world trade. Thus, the finance for a country would give rise to a corresponding array of commodity-contingent liabilities, plus some amount of noncontingent obligations for activities for which contingency is unfeasible.

In effect, securing general developing country obligations can be viewed as creating a "strip" of commodity-contingent claims, each of which is isolated from country-specific sovereign risk. As in the case of many MBSs, by unbundling the risks this way, they can be sold to agents with comparative advantages in bearing these risks at advantageous prices so that their value is greater than when bundled.

The strip concept reinforces the argument for standardization. Thus, given the appropriate third party insurance against default, countries such as Zaire and Peru would both have an interest in issuing standard, copper-contingent bonds (backed by their copper export revenues) with the same payoff profiles, $R(s)$. These securities will appear identical to prospective purchasers, in the same way that the purchaser of a futures contract does not need to know the identity of the seller. Nevertheless, it should be recognized that the insuring body will view these as different risks because the values of future access, $A(s)$, and the penalties, $P(s)$, may be different. In this event, the insurance premia required would differ.

Another possible objection to this proposal is that the developing country sovereign risk is not insurable because it will be highly correlated across countries. The one important reason for this degree of correlation is that developing countries are extremely dependent upon a relatively small group of commodities for their export earnings. As a result, a general depression of commodities has an adverse impact on many countries. Because of this, there is yet further reason for commodity-contingent securities. Once commodity price exposure is split, developing country sovereign risk will be a residual that is more likely to be independent and thus more readily insurable.

It is not only, and perhaps not mainly, governments who will be the issuers of these new insured, contingent securities. In fact, many arrangements appear possible. In many cases, countries may find it effective to decentralize the finance decision and allow specialized enterprises to obtain their own finance and issue liabilities whose contingency matches the enterprise's earnings profile. Alternatively, the borrower might be a private corporation whose ability to borrow is compromised by a perceived threat of nationalization or expropriation. Again, it could be a private commercial bank that would post as collateral a portfolio of (existing or new) developing country loans.

What would be the market for the new securities? Once the sovereign risk insurance is arranged, the success of the issues is largely a function of the abilities of the financiers in designing the payoff profiles and in marketing. These skills have been well developed elsewhere, and there is every reason to think they are applicable here. In particular, commodity-contingent bonds may well behave much like equities of private commodity producers. Consequently, combined with commodity futures and forwards, there may be ample scope for hedging and arbitrage with the consequence that the liquidity of the insured, contingent claims may be quite high.

Finally, it is impossible to state here which institutions are best capable of offering the required sovereign risk insurance. This analysis shows that it is a matter of who can offer a given insurance at the smallest premium. This, in turn, will depend on which institution can extract the greatest penalties, have the biggest impact on future access to finance, and bargain hardest. There is a presumption that this would be a large, very creditworthy institution that has been a long-term participant in international lending. It needs to be emphasized that the insurance described here would be self-financing along actuarial grounds. Consequently, the insuring body could be a private, profit-seeking organization. Most important, no matter whether the insuring body would be private or governmental, the guarantee would not require access to governmental tax revenues.

Notes

1. In 1983, the outstanding value of MBS obligations was $278 billion (Seiders, 1985), a figure comparable to the approximately $249 billion of outstanding nonguaranteed developing country debt (short and long term) in private hands at that time. See the World Bank (1988), pp. 87–88.

2. This describes a "pass-through," such as a Ginnie Mae. Other forms of MBSs strip out the interest and various tranches of principal repayment.

3. In the context of lending to developing country governments and their agencies, these risks would be associated with variability in export earnings, exchange rates, and interest rates.

4. The concept of comparative advantage in bearing diverse types of risks is discussed in Lessard (1986).

5. Later, the contractual payments R will also become state dependent.

6. In the United States, the effect of guaranteeing institutions requiring that MBSs conform to certain standard forms was to create a high degree of standardization, which aided the growth of active secondary trading.

7. This criterion is appropriate for a risk-neutral borrower. Risk aversion or intertemporal consumption smoothing may also be a consideration affecting the supply of securities. Most of the literature on commodity contingency takes this to be the sole objective for contingency. This analysis shows that the facilitation or securitization is another, possibly more significant, consideration in structuring payoffs. In effect, this deals with the demand for securities.

8. If markets are noncompetitive, price-contingent contracts may alter the incentives borrowers face in their production decisions. In this case, the price-contingent contracts may be manipulatable. See Anderson and Sundaresan (1984) and Newbery (1984). More generally, price contingency may affect borrower's investment allocation decisions. See Besley and Powell (1988).

9. Here, the figure has been normalized to allow for a quantity of unity. This is a harmless simplification given that quantity uncertainty is being subtracted in this discussion.

11
Conclusion

Theophilos Priovolos and Ronald C. Duncan

The collection of papers brought together in this volume was written to advance knowledge about the demand, pricing, and use of commodity-linked finance.[1] Fall extended the work of O'Hara on the demand for commodity bonds and showed that the demand function for commodity bonds has two components—a speculative component and a hedging component—and that the demand for commodity bonds is positive when the investor has a lower relative modified risk tolerance than the market, that is, a higher relative modified risk aversion. Rajan simplified the work of Schwartz on the pricing of commodity bonds by introducing the use of binomial pricing theory. Thompson and Myers extended the typical one-period, mean-variance framework for the computation of the optimal commodity hedge ratio by the use of vector autoregression; thus, they were able to capture variations in both export patterns and departures from random walks in commodity prices. Claessens extended the typical optimal hedge methodology to include exchange rate risk, in addition to commodity price risk. Ball and Myers further extended this optimal hedge methodology to a sovereign borrower without any existing debt.

The Wright and Newbery paper quantifies the costs of export revenue variability and the potential for risk reduction through reserve management and commodity hedging and demonstrates the importance of risk management for consumption smoothing. Employing a model of default based on the tradeoff between the borrower's expected future consumption smoothing benefits from external finance and the cost of meeting its obligation, Wright and Newbery show that, with commodity bonds, the probability of default is reduced. Such contracts reveal the "permanent" level of income that the country could count on from its commodity exports.

Anderson, Gilbert, and Powell show that borrowers and lenders do not always have a comparative advantage in hedging all types of risks. They show that the probability of default risk reduces when the contract terms of an obligation are written so that the repayments schedule depends on income. Moral hazard and cost standardization concerns constitute two strong arguments against using "income" such as export earnings. Provided markets are competitive, both difficulties can be circumvented by introducing contingency through internationally quoted price and exchange rates. They show that, for low values of commodity prices, the default penalty and the value of future access to finance are low (if they are a function of commodity prices) and that, beyond a critical commodity price level, developing countries will have an incentive to default.

A standard recommendation has been that when a project faces commodity price uncertainty, it should be protected against the risk of low commodity prices by hedging in forward markets or other similar markets (such as futures, options, swaps, etc.) if they are available. More specifically, by financing through a combination of straight debt and forward sales, this will assure a constant income for the borrower. This strategy does not necessarily assure the incentives to fulfill the contract terms, however. Anderson, Gilbert, and Powell find the likely conditions under which incentives will exist to ensure that the terms of the contract are fulfilled. Several considerations suggest that straight debt combined with forward sales may still not be the best means of assuring that the problem of sovereign risk is substantially reduced.

One problem that arises with this combination is that it generally creates two credit risks, not one. Anderson, Gilbert, and Powell point out that one way around this difficulty is to make the forward contract itself part of the collateral for the debt contract; another way is to combine the payment features of the debt and the forward sale into a single instrument. This would become a commodity-contingent bond. If the default penalty or the value of access does not keep pace with the commodity price, the commodity bond will not necessarily assure that the contract will not be circumvented. It may well be that if a commodity producer can retain the profits of a commodity price boom, the value of future access to credit may not increase and may actually fall as prices rise beyond a certain range. A package to circumvent this problem is a commodity bond that combines a straight debt, the sale of a commodity forward, and the purchase of a commodity call at a strike price higher than that for which it was sold forward.

Clearly, such an instrument could be marketed best by the institution providing insurance at the smallest premium for any residual sovereign risk. This, in turn, will depend on who can extract the greatest penalties, have the biggest impact on future access to finance, and bargain hardest.

There is a presumption that this would be a large, very creditworthy institution, which has been a long-term participant in international lending. It needs to be emphasized that the insurance the three authors describe could be self-financing along actuarial grounds. Consequently, the body could be a profit-seeking organization. There is also the point that the residual guarantee will be significantly less than that required if securitization of straight debt is contemplated. In other words, the institution's capital would be able to finance a greater amount of loans (if they were structured in the commodity-linked form) with the same amount of risk it would have otherwise been willing to assume.

Commodity-linked financings have important advantages in the external financing of developing countries relative to the traditional alternatives of foreign currency denominated, general obligation borrowing, or direct foreign investment. They allow developing countries that are overexposed to particular risks, relative to those in the world economy, to shift these risks to world capital markets on an *ex ante* basis. By contrast, general obligation financing also shifts risk, but only on an *ex post* basis through nonperformance with its attendant deadweight penalties. In contrast with direct investment and other forms of finance that also shift risk on an *ex ante* basis, commodity finance is linked to observable, exogenous outcomes and does not require the same degree of costly monitoring or intrusion of foreign forces into domestic decision making. Commodity price-linked finance is preferable to other forms of indexed finance because moral hazard and standardization considerations work against such other forms.

To sum up, commodity-linked financings have expanded rapidly in the late 1980s, but they have been mainly confined to entities in industrial countries. Creditworthiness questions handicap the developing countries in their access to this type of financing. Unless their credit standing can be enhanced, maybe through a third-party guarantee, many developing countries will find it difficult to have independent access to international financial markets for such finance, and they may have to depend on bilateral and multilateral aid and development agencies for their external funding needs. It is clear that the insurance premium required for such third-party guarantees is minimized when the insuring body has a comparative advantage in bearing sovereign risk and when the contractual terms are contingent on factors affecting the borrower's present and future earnings. Commodity-price-contingent instruments are shown to be the most suitable obligation for the developing country needs.

To achieve better risk management in the commodity-dependent developing countries, the implications for the practices of international development agencies on the basis of the findings of the papers included here are:

- To support, with technical assistance, enhancement of institutional and human resources capacity in developing countries in the area of finance, in particular, in commodity price risk management
- To support better risk management practices in project and program lending in developing countries through technical support and/or appropriately tailored lending
- To support commercial cofinancing with the use of partial guarantees and to make their own loans commodity price-contingent
- To support, in the context of restructuring of commodity-dependent developing countries' debt, the exchange of existing debt for appropriately tailored commodity price-contingent debt
- To institute methods to hedge appropriately the derivative commodity exposure in the financial markets by commodity price-linked financings.

Note

1. We would like to thank Todd Petzel and Donald R. Lessard for their enlightened discussion of several of the contributions in this book when they were presented during the 1988 American Agricultural Economics Association meetings in New York. This chapter incorporates as best as possible their major comments. For more details, see Petzel (1989) and Lessard (1989).

Bibliography

Adler, Michael, and David Simon. 1986. "Exchange Rate Surprises in International Portfolios." *The Journal of Portfolio Management* vol. 12, no. 2 (Winter), pp. 44–53.

Ahamed, Liaquat. 1988. "Liability Management: A Portfolio Manager's Point of View." Paper presented at Trends in International Capital Markets: Implications for Developing Countries, Oxford.

Anderson, R. W., ed. 1984. *The Industrial Organization of Futures Markets.* Lexington, Mass.: Lexington Books.

Anderson, R. W., and J. P. Danthine. 1983. "Hedger Diversity in Futures Markets." *Economic Journal* vol. 93 (June), pp. 370–89.

Anderson, R. W., and S. M. Sundaresan. 1984. "Futures Markets and Monopoly." In R. W. Anderson, ed. *The Industrial Organization of Futures Markets.* Lexington, Mass.: Lexington Books.

Benninga, S., Rafael Eldor, and Itzhak Zilcha. 1985. "Optimal International Hedging in Commodity and Currency Forward Markets." *Journal of International Money and Finance* vol. 4, pp. 537–52.

Besley, Timothy, and A. P. Powell. 1988. "The Role of Commodity Indexed Debt in International Lending." Institute of Economics and Statistics, Oxford University, Oxford; processed.

Binder, B. F., and T. W. F. Lindquist. 1982. "Asset/Liability and Funds Management at U.S. Commercial Banks." Bank Administration Institute, Rolling Meadows.

Black, Fischer, and M. S. Scholes. 1972. "The Valuation of Option Contracts and a Test of Market Efficiency." *Journal of Finance* vol. 17, pp. 399–417.

———. 1973. "The Pricing of Options and Corporate Liabilities." *Journal of Political Economy* vol. 81, pp. 637–59.

Bollerslev, T. B. 1986. "Generalized Autoregressive Conditional Heteroskedasticity." *Journal of Econometrics* vol. 31, pp. 307–27.

———. 1987. "Modelling the Coherence in Short Run Nominal Exchange Rates: A Multivariate Generalized ARCH Model." Northwestern University, Chicago; processed.

Branson, W. H., and L. T. Katseli. 1982. "Currency Baskets and the Real Effective Exchange Rates." In M. Gersovitz, et al. *The Theory and Experience of Economic Development. Essays in Honour of Sir W. Arthur Lewis.* London: George Allen and Unwin.

Breeden, D. T. 1979. "An Intertemporal Asset Pricing Model with Stochastic Consumption and Investment Opportunities." *Journal of Financial Economics* vol. 7, pp. 265–96.

———. 1980. "Consumption Risk in Futures Markets." *Journal of Finance* vol. 35, pp. 503–20.

———. 1981. "Some Common Misconceptions about Futures Trading." Teaching Notes. Stanford University, Palo Alto, Calif.; processed.

———. 1984. "Futures Markets and Commodity Options." *Journal of Economic Theory* vol. 32, no. 2, pp. 275–300.

Brennan, M. J. 1958. "The Supply of Storage." *American Economic Review* vol. 48, no. 1, pp. 50–72.

———. 1986. "The Cost of Convenience and the Pricing of Commodity Contingent Claims." Working Paper CSFM-130. Columbia Business School, New York.

Brennan, M. J., and E. S. Schwartz. 1980. "Analyzing Convertible Bonds." *Journal of Financial and Quantitative Analysis* vol. 25, pp. 907–29.

Brown, S. L. 1985. "Reformulation of the Portfolio Model of Hedging." *American Journal of Agricultural Economics* vol. 67, pp. 508–12.

Budd, Nicholas. 1983. "The Future of Commodity-Indexed Financing." *Harvard Business Review* vol. 61, no. 4, pp. 44–50.

Bulow, Jeremy, and Kenneth Rogoff. 1987. "A Constant Recontracting Model of Sovereign Debt." Social Systems Research Institute, University of Wisconsin, Madison; processed.

———. 1988. "Sovereign Debt: Is to Forgive to Forget?" NBER Working Paper 2623. Cambridge, Mass.: National Bureau of Economic Research.

Campbell, R. B., and S. J. Turnovsky. 1982. "Stabilizing and Welfare Properties of Futures Markets: A Simulation Approach." Working Paper 83. Australian National University, Faculty of Economics and Research School of Social Sciences, pp. 1–41.

———. 1985. "Analysis of the Stabilizing and Welfare Effects of Intervention in Spot and Futures Markets." NBER Working Paper 1698. Cambridge, Mass.: National Bureau of Economic Research, pp. 1–37.

Carr, Peter. 1987. "A Note on the Pricing of Commodity-Linked Bonds." *Journal of Finance* vol. 42, no. 4, pp. 1071–76.

Carter, C. A. 1985. "Hedging Opportunities for Canadian Grains." *Canadian Journal of Agricultural Economics* vol. 33, pp. 37–45.

Claessens, Stijn. 1988. "The Optimal Currency Composition of External Debt." PPR Working Paper 14. World Bank, Washington, D.C.; processed.

Cole, H. L., and Maurice Obstfeld. 1988. "Commodity Trade and International Risk Sharing: How Much Do Financial Markets Matter?" International Economics Research Center Working Paper 11, University of Pennsylvania, Philadelphia.

Cooper, R. N., and J. D. Sachs. 1985. "Borrowing Abroad: The Debtor's Perspective." In G. W. Smith and J. T. Cuddington, eds., *International Debt and the Developing Countries*. Washington, D.C.: World Bank.

Cootner, P. H. 1964. *The Random Character of Stock Market Prices*. Boston: MIT Press.

Cox, J. C., J. E. Ingersoll, and S. A. Ross. 1978. "A Theory of the Term Structure of Interest Rates." Research Paper 468, Stanford University, Palo Alto, Calif.

———. 1981. "The Relation Between Forward Prices and Futures Prices." *Journal of Financial Economics* vol. 9, no. 4, pp. 321–46.

———. 1985. "A Theory of the Term Structure of Interest Rates." *Econometrica* vol. 53, no. 2, pp. 363–407.

Cox, J. C., and S. A. Ross. 1976. "The Valuation of Options for Alternative Stochastic Processes." *Journal of Financial Economics* vol. 3, pp. 145–66.

Cox, J. C., S. A. Ross, and M. Rubinstein. 1979. "Option Pricing: A Simplified Approach." *Journal of Financial Economics* vol. 7, pp. 229–63.

Cumby, R. E., and Maurice Obstfeld. 1984. "International Interest and Price Level Linkages under Flexible Exchange Rates: A Review of Recent Evidence." In John F. O. Bilson and Richard C. Marston, eds. *Exchange Rate Theory and Practice*. University of Chicago Press.

Danthine, J. P. 1978. "Information, Futures Prices and Stabilizing Speculation." *Journal of Economic Theory* vol. 17, pp. 79–98.

Dieffenbach, B. C. 1976. "A Theory of Securities Markets under Uncertainty." *Review of Economic Studies* vol. 23, no. 2, pp. 317–27.

Dornbusch, Rudiger. 1980. "Exchange Rate Economics: Where Do We Stand?" *Brookings Papers on Economic Activity* no. 1, pp. 143–94.

———. 1985. "Policy and Performance Links between LDC Debtors and Industrial Nations." *Brookings Papers on Economic Activity* no. 2, pp. 303–56.

———. 1987. "Exchange Rates and Prices." *American Economic Review* vol. 77, pp. 93–106.

Dreyfus, S. E. 1965. *Dynamic Programming and the Calculus of Variations*. New York: Academic Press.

Dunn, K. B., and J. J. McDonnell. 1981. "Valuation of GNMA Mortgage-Backed Securities." *Journal of Finance* vol. 36, no. 2, pp. 471–84.

Dusak, Katherine. 1973. "Futures Trading and Investor Returns: An Investigation of Commodity Market Risk Premiums." *Journal of Political Economy* vol. 81, pp. 1387–1406.

Eaton, Jonathan, and Mark Gersovitz. 1981. "Debt with Potential Repudiation: Theoretical and Empirical Analysis." *Reveiw of Economic Studies* vol. 48, pp. 289–309.

Eaton, Jonathan, Mark Gersovitz, and J. E. Stiglitz. 1986. "The Pure Theory of Country Risk." *European Economic Review* vol. 30, pp. 481–513.

Eichengreen, Barry. 1987. "Til Debt Do Us Part: The U.S. Capital Market and Foreign Lending: 1920–1955." NBER Working Paper 2394. Cambridge, Mass.: National Bureau of Economic Research.

Eldor, Rafael, and David Pines. 1985. "Determinants of the Household Demand for Hedging Instruments." Foerder Institute for Economic Research, Working Paper 1-85, Tel Aviv University, pp. 1–26.

Engle, R. F. 1982. "Autoregressive Conditional Heteroskedasticity with Estimates of the Variance of U.K. Inflation." *Econometrica* vol. 50, pp. 987–1008.

Engle, R. F., and T. B. Bollerslev. 1986. "Modelling the Persistence of Conditional Variances." *Econometric Reviews* vol. 5, pp. 1–50.

Engle, R. F., and C. W. J. Granger. 1977. "Co-integration and Error Correction: Representation, Estimation, and Testing." *Econometrica* vol. 55, pp. 251–76.

Evans, Paul. 1988. "Are Consumers Ricardian? Evidence for the United States." *Journal of Political Economy* vol. 96, pp. 903–1004.

Evnine, Jeremy. 1983. "Three Essays in the Use of Option Pricing Theory." PhD. Thesis. University of California, Berkeley; processed.

Fall, M. A. 1986. "Commodity-Indexed Bonds." Masters Thesis. Sloan School of Management, MIT, Cambridge, Mass.; processed.

Feder, Gershon, and R. E. Just. 1977. "A Study of Debt Servicing Capacity Applying Logit Analysis." *Journal of Development Economics*, vol. 4, no. 1, pp. 25–32.

Finger, J. M., and D. A. de Rosa. 1980. "The Compensatory Finance Facility and Export Instability." *Journal of World Trade Law* vol. 14, pp. 14–22.

Fischer, Stanley. 1975. "The Demand for Index Bonds." *Journal of Political Economy* vol. 83, pp. 509–34.

———. 1978. "Call Option Pricing When the Exercise Price Is Uncertain and the Valuation of Index Bonds." *Journal of Finance* vol. 33, no. 1, pp. 169–76.

Fishlow, Albert. 1987. "Lessons of the 1880's for the 1980's." Working Paper 8724. University of California, Berkeley, Department of Economics.

Flood, Eugene, Jr. 1986. "An Empirical Analysis of the Effect of Exchange Rate Changes on Goods Prices." Graduate School of Business Administration, Stanford University, April; processed.

Frankel, J. A. 1981. "Flexible Exchange Rates, Prices and the Role of 'News': Lessons from the 1970s." *Journal of Political Economy* vol. 89, pp. 665–705.

———. 1983. "Estimation of Portfolio-Balance Functions That Are Mean-Variance Optimizing." *European Economic Review* vol. 23, pp. 315–27.

Gemmill, G. T. 1980. "The Effectiveness of Hedging and the Variance of Spot and Futures Prices." City University Business School, London; processed.

———. 1985. "Optimal Hedging on Futures Markets for Commodity-Exporting Nations." *European Economic Review* vol. 27, pp. 243–61.

Gersovitz, Mark. 1983. "Trade, Capital Mobility and Sovereign Immunity." Discussion Paper 108. Research Program in Development Studies, Princeton University.

———. 1985. "Banks' International Lending Decisions: What We Know and Implications for Future Research." In Gordon W. Smith and John T. Cuddington, eds. *International Debt and the Developing Countries.* Washington, D.C.: World Bank.

Gilbert, C. L. 1988. "The Impact of Exchange Rates and Developing Country Debt on Commodity Prices." *Economic Journal* vol. 99, pp. 773–84.

Giovannini, Alberto. 1985. "Exchange Rates and Traded Goods Prices." Graduate School of Business, Columbia University, New York; processed.

Gordon-Ashworth, Fiona. 1984. *International Commodity Control: A Contemporary History and Appraisal.* London: Croom Helm.

Goss, B. A., and B. S. Yamey, eds. 1978. *The Economics of Futures Trading.* London: Macmillan.

Grossman, H. I., and J. B. van Huyck. 1985. "Sovereign Debt as an Contingent Claim, Excusable Default, Repudiation and Reputation," NBER Working Paper 1673. Cambridge, Mass.: National Bureau of Economic Research.

Hansen, L. P., and T. S. 1980. "Formulating and Estimating Dynamic Linear Rational Expectations Models." *Journal of Economic Dynamics and Control* vol. 2, pp. 7–46.

Haslem, J. A. 1984. *Bank Funds Management: Text and Readings.* Reston, N.J.: Reston Publishing Company.

Hazuka, T. B. 1984. "Consumption Betas and Backwardation in Commodity Markets." *Journal of Finance* vol. 39, pp. 647–55.

Heifner, R. G. 1978. "Minimum Risk Pre-Harvest Sales of Soybeans." National Economic Analysis Division, U.S. Department of Agriculture, Washington, D.C.

Holthausen, Duncan. 1979. "Hedging and the Competitive Firm Under Price Uncertainty." *American Economic Review* vol. 69, pp. 989–95.

Ingersoll, J. E., Jr. 1982. "The Pricing of Commodity-Linked Bonds, Discussion." *Journal of Finance* vol. 37, no. 2, pp. 540–41.

Ito, Kiyoshi, and H. P. McKean. 1964. *Diffusion Processes and Their Sample Paths*. New York: Academic Press.

Johnson, L. L. 1960. "The Theory of Hedging and Speculation in Commodity Futures." *Review of Economic Studies* vol. 27, pp. 139–51.

Jones, Terry. 1984. "Growing World of Commodity Finance." *Euromoney Trade Finance Report* vol. 13, pp. 29–30.

Joskow, P. L. 1977. "Commercial Impossibility: The Uranium Market and the Westinghouse Case." *Journal of Legal Studies* vol. 6, pp. 119–76.

Kantor, L. G. 1986. "Inflation Uncertainty and Real Economic Activity: An Alternative Approach." *Review of Economics and Statistics* vol. 68, pp. 493–500.

Karp, Larry. 1986. "Dynamic Hedging with Uncertain Production." Working Paper 371. University of California, Division of Agricultural Sciences, pp. 1–25.

Keynes, J. M. 1924. "Foreign Investment and the National Advantage." *The Nation and Athenaeum*.

Kinney, J. M., and R. T. Garrigan, eds. 1985. *The Handbook of Mortgage Banking*. Homewood, Ill.: Dow Jones-Irwin.

Kletzer, K. M. 1988. "Sovereign Debt Renegotiation Under Asymmetric Information." Discussion Paper 555. Yale University Economic Growth Center, New Haven, Conn.

Koppenhaver, G. D. 1984. "Variable-Rate Loan Commitments, Deposit Withdrawal Risk, and Anticipatory Hedging." Federal Reserve Bank of Chicago, Staff Memoranda sm-85-6, pp. 1–26.

Korsvik, W. J., and C. O. Meiburg. 1986. *The Loan Officer's Handbook*. Homewood, Ill.: Dow Jones-Irwin.

Kraft, D. F., and R. F. Engle. 1982. "Autoregressive Conditional Heteroskedasticity in Multiple Time Series Models." Discussion Paper 82-23. University of California, San Diego.

Kroner, Kenneth, and Stijn Claessens. 1988. "Improving the Currency Composition of External Debt: Applications in Indonesia and Turkey." PPR Working Paper 150. World Bank, Washington, D.C.; processed.

Lessard, D. R. 1977a. "Commodity-Linked Bonds from Less-Developed Countries: An Investment Opportunity." MIT, Cambridge, Mass.; processed.

———. 1977b. "Risk Efficient External Financing Strategies for Commodity Producing Countries." MIT, Cambridge, Mass.; processed.

———. 1979. "Risk Efficient External Financing for Commodity Producing Developing Countries: A Progress Report." MIT, Cambridge, Mass.; processed.

———. 1980. "Financial Mechanisms for Stabilizing Revenues of Commodity Producing Developing Countries: Narrative Report." Sloan School of Management, MIT, Cambridge, Mass.; processed.

———. 1986. "The Management of International Trade Risks." *The Geneva Papers on Risk and Insurance* vol. 11, pp. 255–64.

———. 1987. "Recapitalizing Third-World Debt: Toward a New Vision of Commercial Financing for Less-Developed Countries." *Midland Corporate Finance Journal* vol. 5, pp. 6–21.

———. 1989. "Financial Risk Management Needs of Developing Countries: Discussion." *American Journal of Agricultural Economics* vol. 71, no. 2 (May), pp. 534–35.

Lessard, D. R., and John Williamson. 1985. *Financial Intermediation Beyond the Debt Crisis.* Washington, D.C.: Institute for International Economics.

Leuthold, R. M., and P. A. Hartmann. 1979. "A Semi-Strong Form Evaluation of the Efficiency of the Hog Futures Market." *American Journal of Agricultural Economics* vol. 61, pp. 482–89.

Lindert, P. H., and P. J. Morton. 1987. "How Sovereign Debt Has Worked." Macro Policy Working Paper Series 45. University of California-Davis, Institute of Government Affairs Research Program in Applied Macroeconomics, Davis, Calif.

Lipschitz, Leslie, and V. Sundararajan. 1982. "The Optimal Basket in a World of Generalized Floating." *IMF Staff Papers*, pp. 80–100.

Long, J. B. 1974. "Stock Prices, Inflation and the Term Structure of Interest Rates." *Journal of Financial Economics* vol. 1, no. 2, pp. 131–70.

Madura, Jeff, and Reiff Wallace. 1985. "Hedge Strategy for International Porfolios." *Journal of Portfolio Management* vol. 12, pp. 70–74.

Markham, J. W., and K. K. Bergin. 1985. "The Role of the Commodity Futures Trading Commission in International Commodity Transactions." *George Washington Journal of International Law and Economics* vol. 18, pp. 581–629.

Markowitz, H. M. 1952. "Portfolio Selection." *Journal of Finance* vol. 7, pp. 77–91.

Mason, S. P., and R. C. Merton. 1985. "The Role of Contingent Claims Analysis in Corporate Finance." In E. Altman and M. Subrahmanyam, eds. *Recent Advances in Corporate Finance.* Homewood, Ill.: R. D. Irwin.

McCarthy, David and Robert Palache. 1986. "Eurobonds, Bells and Whistles: How Issues Were Structured." *International Financial Law Review* vol. 5, no. 6, pp. 27–32.

McDonald, Robert, and Daniel Siegel. 1984. "Option Pricing When the Under-lying Asset Earns a Below-Equilibrium Rate of Return: A Note." *Journal of Finance* vol. 39, no. 1, pp. 261–65.

McFadden, R. T. 1984. "Energy Futures Contracts and the Uses in Countertrade/ Barter Deals." *Countertrade & Barter Quarterly* vol. 4, pp. 47–50.

McKean, H. P. 1969. *Stochastic Integral*. New York: Academic Press.

McKinney, G. W., and W. J. Brown. 1974. *Management of Commercial Bank Funds*. New York: American Institute of Banking.

McKinnon, R. I. 1967. "Futures Markets, Buffer Stocks, and Income Stability for Primary Producers." *Journal of Political Economy* vol. 75, pp. 844–61.

Merrill Lynch. 1978. *The Merrill Lynch Guide to Speculating in Commodity Futures*. New York.

Merton, R. C. 1969. "Lifetime Portfolio Selection Under Uncertainty: The Continuous-Time Case." *Review of Economic Statistics* vol. 51, no. 3, pp. 247–57.

———. 1971. "Optimum Consumption and Portfolio Rules in a Continuous Time Model." *Journal of Economic Theory* vol. 3, pp. 373–413.

———. 1973a. "An Intertemporal Capital Asset Pricing Model." *Econometrics* vol. 41, pp. 867–87.

———. 1973b. "Theory of Rational Option Pricing." *Bell Journal of Economics and Management Science, vol. 4, pp. 141–83.*

Meyer, Jack. 1987. "Two-Moment Decision Models and Expected Utility Maximization." *The American Economic Review* vol. 77, pp. 421–30.

Meyer, Jack, and L. J. Robison. 1988. "Hedging and Price Randomness." *American Journal of Agricultural Economics* vol. 70, pp. 268–80.

Newbery, D. M. G. 1984. "The Manipulation of Futures Markets by a Dominant Producer." In R. W. Anderson, ed., *The Industrial Organization of Futures Markets*. Lexington, Mass.: Lexington Books.

Newbery, D. M. G., and J. E. Stiglitz. 1981. "The Theory of Commodity Price Stabilization." Oxford: Oxford University Press.

O'Hara, Maureen. 1984. "Commodity Bonds and Consumption Risks." *Journal of Finance* vol. 39, pp. 193–206.

Page, S. A. 1981. "The Choice of Invoicing Currencies in Merchandise Trade." *National Institute Economic Review* vol. 81, pp. 60–72.

Peck, A. E. 1975. "Hedging and Income Stability: Concepts, Implications, and an Example." *American Journal of Agricultural Economics* vol. 57, pp. 410–19.

Petzel, T. E. 1989. "Financial Risk Management Needs of Developing Countries: Discussion." *American Journal of Agricultural Economics* vol. 71, no. 2 (May), pp. 531–33.

Pindyck, R. S. 1983. "Cartel and Oligopolistic Pricing." Lecture Notes, Sloan School of Management, MIT, Cambridge, Mass.; processed.

Powell, A. P., and C. L. Gilbert. 1988. "The Use of Commodity Contingent Contracts in the Management of Developing Country Debt Risk." In D. Currie and D. Vines, eds. *Macroeconomic Interactions Between North and South.* Cambridge: Cambridge University Press.

Powers, M. J., and David Vogel. 1984. *Inside the Financial Futures Markets.* New York: John Wiley & Sons.

Priovolos, Theophilos. 1987a. "Commodity Bonds: A Risk Management Instrument for Developing Countries." IECCM Working Paper 1987-12. World Bank, Washington, D.C.; processed.

————. 1987b. "An Overview of Commodity Bonds: A Balance Sheet Management Instrument." IECCM, World Bank, Washington, D.C.; processed.

Richard, S. F., and S. M. Sundaresan. 1981. "A Continuous Time Equilibrium Model of Forward Prices and Futures Prices in a Multigood Economy." *Journal of Financial Economics* vol. 9, pp. 347–71.

Rolfo, Jacques. 1980. "Optimal Hedging under Price and Quantity Uncertainty: The Case of a Cocoa Producer." *Journal of Political Economy* vol. 88, pp. 100–16.

Sachs, Jeffrey, and Daniel Cohen. 1982. "LDC Borrowing with Default Risk." NBER Working Paper 925. Cambridge, Mass.: National Bureau of Economic Research.

Samuelson, P. A. 1985. "The Public Interest and Commerical Advantage of a Mechanism to Hedge against Inflation Risks." MIT, Cambridge, Mass.; processed.

Sarris, A. H. 1984. "Speculative Storage, Futures Markets, and the Stability of Commodity Prices." *Economic Inquiry* vol. 22, pp. 80–97.

Schwartz, E. S. 1982. "The Pricing of Commodity Bonds." *Journal of Finance* vol. 37, pp. 525–39.

Seiders, D. F. 1985. "Residential Mortgage and Capital Markets." In *The Handbook of Mortgage Banking.* Homewood, Ill.: Dow Jones-Irwin.

Shapiro, A. C. 1984. "Currency Risk and Relative Price Risk." *Journal of Financial and Quantitative Analysis* vol. 19, pp. 365–73.

Sharpe, W. F. 1964. "Capital Asset Prices: A Theory of Market Equilibrium Under Conditions of Risk." *Journal of Finance* vol. 19, no. 3, pp. 425–42.

————. 1981. *Investment.* Englewood Cliffs, N.J.: Prentice-Hall.

Sims, C. A. 1980. "Macroeconomics and Reality." *Econometrica* vol. 48, pp. 1–48.

Smirlock, M. 1986. "Hedging Bank Borrowing Costs with Financial Futures." Federal Reserve Bank of Philadelphia, *Business Review*, pp. 13–23.

Smith, C. W. 1976. "Option Pricing: A Review." *Journal of Financial Economics* vol. 3, pp. 1–51.

Smith, C. W. 1978a. "Commodity Instability and Market Failure: A Survey of Issues." In F. G. Adams and S. Klein, eds. *Stabilizing World Commodity Markets.* Lexington, Mass.: Lexington Books.

———. 1978b. *Numerical Solutions of Partial Differential Equations.* Oxford: Oxford University Press.

Smith, C. W., and R. M. Stulz. 1985. "Determinants of Firms' Hedging Policies." *Journal of Financial and Quantitative Analysis* vol. 20, pp. 391–405.

Srinivasan, Bobby, and Anant Negandhi. 1985. "Hedging in Currency Futures: A Singapore Dollar Case Study." *Asia Pacific Journal of Management* vol. 2, pp. 170–79.

Stapleton, R. C., and M. G. Subrahmanyam. 1984. "The Valuation of Multivariate Contingent Claims in Discrete Time Models." *Journal of Finance* vol. 39, no. 1, pp. 207–29.

Stein, J. L. 1961. "The Simultaneous Determination of Spot and Futures Prices." *American Economic Review* vol. 51, pp. 1012–25.

Stone, R. 1989. "Financing COMINCO's Red Dog Project." Fifth Mineral Economics Symposium, Toronto, Ontario.

Stulz, R. M. 1981. "A Model of International Pricing." *Journal of Financial Economics* vol. 9, pp. 383–406.

———. 1982. "Options on the Minimum or the Maximum of Two Risky Assets." *Journal of Financial Economics* vol. 10, no. 2, pp. 161–85.

———. 1984. "Optimal Hedging Policies." *Journal of Financial and Quantitative Analysis* vol. 19, pp. 127–40.

Svensson, L. E. O. 1987. "Optimal Foreign Debt Composition." World Bank, Washington, D.C., December; processed.

———. 1988. "Portfolio Choice and Asset Pricing with Nontraded Assets." Institute for International Economics, University of Stockholm, July; processed.

Tesler, L. G. 1981. "Why There Are Organized Futures Markets." *The Journal of Law and Economics.* vol. 24, no. 1, pp. 1–22.

Thygerson, K. J. 1985. "Federal Government-Related Mortgage Purchasers." In *The Handbook of Mortgage Banking.* Homewood, Ill.: Dow Jones-Irwin.

Van Horme, J. C. 1980. *Financial Market Rates and Flows.* Englewood Cliffs, N.J.: Prentice Hall Inc.

Varangis, Panos, and R. C. Duncan. 1990. "The Response of Japanese and U.S. Steel Prices to Changes in the Yen-Dollar Exchange Rate." WPS 367. World Bank, Washington, D.C.; processed.

Webb, S. B., and H. S. Zia. 1989. "Borrowings, Resource Transfers, and External Shocks to Developing Countries: Historical and Counterfactual." PPR Working Paper 235. World Bank, Washington, D.C.; processed.

Wells, R. 1989. "Optimal Diversification in International Borrowing." Department of Economics, University of California, Berkeley, January; processed.

Williamson, John. 1982. "A Survey of the Literature on the Optimal Peg." *Journal of Development Economics* vol. 11, pp. 39–62.

Woodward, P. 1989. "Trends in Gold Lending to Gold Mining Companies." Fifth Mineral Economics Symposium, Toronto, Ontario.

Working, Holbrook. 1953. "Futures Trading and Hedging." *American Economic Review* vol. 43, pp. 314–43.

World Bank. 1984. *Borrowing and Lending Technology: A World Bank Glossary.* Washington, D.C.

———. 1988a. *Commodity Trade and Price Trends.* Washington, D.C.

———. 1988b. "Financial Flows to Developing Countries." IECDI. Washington, D.C.; processed.

———. 1988c. *World Debt Tables 1987–88, First Supplement.* Washington, D.C.

Worrall, Tim. 1987. "Debt with Potential Repudiation: Short-Run and Long-Run Contracts." University of Reading Discussion Papers in Economics, Series A, no. 186.

Wright, B. D., and J. C. Williams. 1982. "The Economic Role of Commodity Storage." *Economic Journal* vol. 92, pp. 596–614.

Index